Keep
Your Business
Close . . .

and

Your Family
Closer

*Building on the Inherent Strengths
of Family Businesses*

Larry Hollar

Piñon Publishing
Pueblo, Colorado

Requests for permission should be addressed to:

Piñon Publishing
140 West 29th Street, #197
Pueblo, Colorado 81008
866-851-6305

ISBN 0-9766659-0-5

Printed in the United States of America

Cover and interior illustrations by Zachary Howard.

To my family

Family Business Forum

Acknowledgments

I gratefully acknowledge all the people mentioned in this book for their friendship and for their training. Whether friends, family, or business associates, you have inspired me.

Thanks to Tom Cody for being a friend and leader.

This book would not have been started, continued or finished without the mentorship of my editor and coach, Dawn DiPrince of Piñon Publishing. Thank you, Dawn!

Thanks, Dad, for more expert business advice than can be measured. Mom, your love shines through all of your children and grandchildren. I love you both.

My wife Helen Hollar helped to shape and improve this book. Your wisdom, Helen, is a marvel to me.

Acknowledgments

I gratefully acknowledge all the people mentioned in this book for their friendship and for their training. Whether friends, family, or business associates, you have inspired me.

Thanks to Tom Cody for being a friend and leader.

This book would not have been started, continued or finished without the mentorship of my editor and coach, Dawn DiPrince of Piñon Publishing. Thank you, Dawn!

Thanks, Dad, for more expert business advice than can be measured. Mom, your love shines through all of your children and grandchildren. I love you both.

My wife Helen Hollar helped to shape and improve this book. Your wisdom, Helen, is a marvel to me.

Table of Contents

"Work is love made visible.
And if you cannot work with love
but only with distaste,
it is better that
you should leave your work."
— Khalil Gibran

CHAPTER ONE

Leveraging Your Advantages

My great-grandfather drove a stagecoach and was a cowboy until age 39 when he married. He worked in several states of the Old West, but eventually settled down in Kansas. He fathered eight children, including my great-uncle Merl Axford Rosel.

Another ancestor settled in Wisconsin, and his name was Axford. He had a bureau made out of cherry wood that has been handed down five generations to me, since my middle name is Axford too.

Knowledge continues for generations whether you realize it or not. Whether your background is Bedouin, American pioneer, Dutch or Samurai, you will carry forward some characteristics. For example in my case, Axfords learn how to juggle.

My great uncle Merl took me out in his backyard one day and asked, "Do you know how to juggle?" As I tried to explain that it was impossible and that I was only nine years old, Merl picked up a tomato from the garden, a baseball and a gourd. The gourd was the size and shape of an orange, it grew as a weed along the roadside. He held

two spheres in his right hand, one in his left. He
tossed one from his right hand into the air, before it
could land, released the ball from his left hand, and
repeated the action with his right hand. At all times
at least two balls were in the air. I was eager to give
this a try. I was given the three items, tossed them
once and all three fell to the ground.

"I can't do this," I whined. "Well, you can't do it
at first," Uncle Merl explained, "but you learn by
starting with one ball in one hand. Just toss it up a
foot or two, catch it in the same hand."

I could more or less do that. He, then, gave me a
second ball, telling me to do the same thing but
with both. I could do that a time or two before drop-
ping them. Uncle Merl said "You just practice with
that gourd and tomato for a while and later on I'll
show you how to add the baseball."

So, I practiced and practiced with two spheres
and one hand. This went on for days, and I wore
out several tomatoes. Later in my two-week visit to
Lakin, Kansas, Uncle Merl showed me how to add
the baseball and the left hand. "Just practice a while,
you'll get better." Before I got home I could juggle,
and I still enjoy it.

While I still juggle occasionally for pleasure, my
professional life is full of juggling a family business.
Would you care to learn how to juggle in your family
business? If a nine-year-old can learn how to juggle a
tomato, a gourd and a baseball, you can learn how
to maintain balance among family, business and

ownership. Family businesses have advantages over other businesses, and each of these advantages can be leveraged for profit, fun and growth.

MY POINT OF VIEW

Our business-family has been making the transition from the founding generation into the second generation of managers for 30 years. The founder of our business, my father Vic, bought a 50-year-old seed company in 1950. Vic is not only still alive, but is present in the office building almost daily. Not enough good things can be said about him: His courage to start the business and his leadership ability over the past five decades.

My two brothers, Jim and Andy, have worked in the business for many years. Jim Hollar has been the genius behind new product development; his products have kept us afloat. Andy Hollar is the only one of the three who garnered considerable outside experience before joining the company. His expertise in computers, photography and engineering have been invaluable. While they are older, I have been the company president for nearly 30 years. While I am the nominal president, we have a very collaborative way of making decisions. The leadership group includes family and non-family staff members.

My sister, Kitty Overmyer, has never been on staff in our company, but she is a big supporter. She is about to move back to our little town, Rocky Ford, Colorado where she will have an important role as an emotional leader. As I write, the first member of the third generation is deciding whether to join the firm.

The business is extremely small by industry standards, but large compared to most family businesses in our rural community. Our business produces and exports vegetable seed. We have a team of professional plant breeders who develop improved hybrid watermelon, melon, squash and cucumber varieties. While it is hard to imagine millions of dollars worth of such seed for planting, our sales are in the millions annually, grabbing only a minor share of the global market. We compete against conglomerates domestically and in over 50 countries. These industry giants are made up of hundreds of businesses that used to be like ours. Family businesses do make up a portion of the seed industry, and some of those are extremely large compared to us.

Our ownership structure is closely held, while non-family members have long been shareholders. We have eight shareholders, none of which has owned more than 50% for many years. The business operates as a regular corporation.

Exporting to 50 countries has given me the opportunity to meet many wonderful people around the world. We have a joint venture company in China, and our seed is produced on four continents. My best friends are in their own family businesses. In our industry we support each other. As I travel, I always turn the discussion towards management of business and cooperation of family. These discussions have taken me inside several companies as an informal consultant. What an honor it can be to peek under the calm surface at the inner machinery.

I have long been a student of the science of family business management. Starting at age 30, my lessons came from both reading the academic texts and on-the-job training. It has been my passionate hobby for nearly 25 years.

When talking to our son-in-law about joining the business, I went to my bookshelf to get him the best book on the business family dynamic. While I can rate them from best to worst, I couldn't find the one book to help him learn and to make his decision. So I decided to write that book.

I prefer to work from the positive point of view, because there are so many benefits to spending your adult life with your family, knowing that the work you do benefits the group. *Keep Your Business Close, and Your Family Closer* is for all family members and all non-family staff, not just the bosses.

No business on earth is exactly the same as Hollar Seeds, nor is any business exactly like yours. The possible combinations of ownership structure, management styles, and family personalities are endless.

So, you may ask the question: How valuable can my opinion be to you? The bookshelf on family business management is unsatisfying because there are not enough answers, not enough opinions. So I'll give my opinion, along with this warning: Ultimately, you have to make the tough decisions.

LEVERAGE YOUR ADVANTAGES

While reading this book, notice the advantages at work in your business. Use them as leverage for improvement. Increase and improve upon communication. Connect with other family business people. We have common problems, and your friends might have already solved the one you have now. Families think and plan for the long term; that is their nature. Take advantage of multi-generational planning. Improve your business's culture by molding it around your healthy family. Base your business actions on the values that your family holds dear.

USING THE "ADVANTAGE MODEL"

Think of your participation in a family firm as a rapidly changing set of interpersonal relationships. Some of these relationships are between you and other family members. But some relationships are between you and the business. Business ideas are constantly appearing, and your responsibilities can change.

Imagine that your work life is like a circus trick. The tightrope walker could be anyone in the business. It could be the founder or second-generation president. It could be the newly hired nephew or niece. The board of directors is a tightrope walker

**WORKING IN A FAMILY BUSINESS
CAN BE LIKE A CIRCUS TRICK.**

for sure. But no matter which entity is walking the tightrope of life, there is some juggling going on.

THE FAMILY. Uncle Merl's tomato had the ability to change from green to pink to red, from hard to soft. In the same way, the family changes. The founder passes from youth to middle age to retirement age. Sons and daughters pass through stages. During these stages, sons and daughters consider entering the business, working within it, becoming owner/managers. The older the company, the more likely it is that cousins will work together. The older the company, the more likely it is that people from three generations will be working side by side.

Family members evolve from entering the business to working together to passing the baton. Your role in the family, your role in the business, your role as owner will change, as will the roles of the people you work with. Employed children become coworkers, then they become bosses. Bosses might become dependents. Who would you rather depend upon than family during such complex and emotional times?

Even if the business was started with only one person in it, soon enough other family members will be checking it out, helping after school. Before you know it, sons and daughters that aren't even in the business may be wondering about profit sharing. In what seems to be a blink of the eye, the founder will want to train an understudy. The founder will want to fund a retirement.

THE BUSINESS. A business is an entity of its own, like a person. It pays taxes. It has good years and bad. Like a ball being juggled, it's constantly on the move. Up or down. Around and around. A business also evolves from one stage to another. Companies change from *start-up* to *expansion* to *maturity*. From maturity it can reinvent, revitalize or begin to die. Do you see the natural advantage of putting family and business together? Every generation has the chance to reinvent the business. In fact, each generation has the *responsibility* to reinvent the business.

The evolution may take a long time, or it can happen quickly. A grocery store may remain in more or less the same situation for generations, while a high-tech start-up may flame out in 15 years. While the steady, stable grocery store may keep the same building in the same location, sales can begin to drop when it reaches maturity. It is up to the younger generation to fill it with modern goods — to reinvent the look, or to change from cash registers to computers with bar code reading ability.

OWNERSHIP. Generally speaking ownership evolves from simple to complex as more generations become owners. Instead of ownership resting with one or two founders, ownership tends to go to more people as shares are given to children. Ownership questions are key in business planning. They are not discussed as frequently as business and family matters, yet from a multi-generational perspective, the ownership

17

ball is in motion. Ownership and emotions tied to ownership are crucial issues. Chapter 11 will show the advantage of open discussion of ownership.

WHAT IS JUGGLING?

Juggling is the constant attention to business, ownership and family. Juggling is paying attention to each ball when it is time to pay attention to it. Juggling is doing something to one ball depending on what the other two are doing.

For example, there was a week when our ownership team was considering a change to the corporate bylaws. This led to discussion on the Articles of Incorporation and the Stock Restriction Agreement. This area is confined to owners, and we were focused on that ball. By the end of the week we had to change our focus to the business ball, to interview my son in law for a position in the company. When I went home that night, out came the family ball as my wife and I discussed the potential move of our daughter from Nebraska to Colorado. While concentrating on the balls of ownership and family, a large sale emerged pulling our attention from family and ownership matters back into a strictly business question.

HOW DOES THE TIGHT ROPE WALKER HANDLE ALL THIS? There are times when he can't. He then relies on the *safety net* to catch him if he falls, or to catch the balls as they drop. You have built your safety net for years. It includes family members who have been educated about the business. It includes the *emotional leader* of your family. The net includes non-family staff who step in at the time of need. There is a list of tools in Chapter 10, they are a big part of the safety net. The important thing is to use this safety net, then to climb back onto the tightrope of life to start juggling again.

There will be tough weeks. Business problems abound. It is much better to be handling them with family around, in an environment where you have loving support, than to have the same weeks while working for someone else.

You can trust me on this. I've been through 30 years of small heart breaks, of near desperation, of complications, of gut-wrenching family dilemmas, and I wouldn't have missed it for the world.

Part of maintaining your balance on the tightrope is dividing your life into business, self, family and community service. If you are working 80 hours a week and ignoring your school age children, you'll tilt to the right and fall off. If you are on four school committees, attending all the extra-curricular activities while ignoring vital work, you lean too far to the left and fall off the tightrope. Examine your time and fill in the pie chart on the next page.

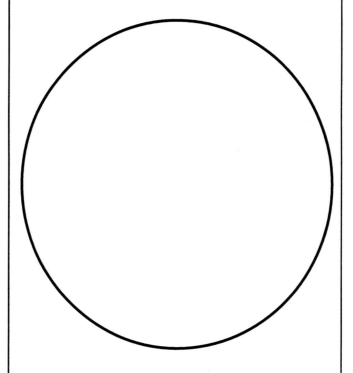

HOW BALANCED ARE YOU?

DIRECTIONS: Create your own pie chart. Determine how much time and energy you devote to each of the following items: Self, Family, Work, Community Service. Draw a pie wedge in the circle above to represent the percentage of your life spent on each thing. (Remember, it altogether should equal 100%.) Please be honest with yourself. How balanced are you?

Are you taking vacations? Are you doing things with your children and with the extended family? Are you irritable with family members and coworkers? If so, take some more personal time. Get into yoga, exercise, or reading. You can't walk a tightrope if you don't have balance. You won't enjoy life if you concentrate too much on one thing.

The Advantage Model is a juggler walking a tightrope. But remember, a model is only a representation. The map is not the country. Models are more useful for teaching than for learning. The reality of your business, family and ownership situation is even more complex, yet immensely more simple than this model. Simple because when the family is healthy, when things are in balance, working in a family business is easy.

Once a neighboring family business leader and his son asked if we could lunch together. They wanted to ask about my experience in China. Since we didn't know each other, we started lunch while describing our businesses. The father asked "Is your little seed business profitable enough to support the four nuclear families?" I replied that so far it was. "Well, God help you when it isn't." While those words have been ringing in my ears for several years, I don't think family businesses are more threatened during economic strife than any other business. Just the opposite, in fact.

Our industry went through a severe downturn starting four years ago. Our sales dropped by 40%. Yet we did not lay off one staff member. We tightened our belts. We worked together as a family. We told everyone on staff the situation. I think that only because we had a strong culture of loyalty, honesty and affection we were able to turn things around. That strong culture is based upon family values more than it is based upon wise business practices. And it works.

Old family business proverb:
"*Not everything
that looks good on paper
is worth the paper
it looks good on.*"

CHAPTER TWO

Joining the Family Business

Should you join the family business? A family business has a lot of advantages, and this book shows you how to put them to use for fun, profit and togetherness. If you are considering this question, please read all of this book. It was all written with you in mind. Multi-generational friendships are a very big springboard for your career. One main consideration is: Where else can you find the kind of support that you have within a healthy family?

If your family isn't so sociable and healthy, perhaps you liken joining the family business to swimming with sharks. That's okay, what greater calling can there be than changing a less than healthy family into a healthy one? That can be part of your contribution. It's better to be around family than to be employed by outsiders. You, as the latest hire, can make the difference.

On the other hand, you often hear the advice to follow your passion. If the family business is plastering and you are an artist, consider being an artist. But factor in the financial safety of being a plaster master versus the financial outlook of the artist. I know a professional baseball player that is a plumber with his brothers in the off season. Which one is his passion? I know which is more glamorous, but I don't know which he is passionate about, or even, which is more profitable. No doubt, he's very lucky to have both.

Realize that when you work in the family firm, what you do benefits your nuclear family and your extended family. Celebrate the fact that your work isn't just for some fat cat back at corporate headquarters. Become passionate about your product or service. Become passionate about making your workplace an enjoyable place. Become passionate about improving family relationships.

> *Realize that when you work
> in the family firm, what you do
> benefits your nuclear family
> and your extended family.*

Whether you are an actual shareholder or not, you have *ownership*. The family firm is the place for your ideas and talents. What is the difference between running a cash register for your uncle and running one for a conglomerate? Your friendliness and efficiency bring customers back, they benefit the company owner. Your honesty adds to profits. Your ideas for improvement improve the company. In a family business, you have a better chance of harvesting some of the good that you do.

Knowing that what you do at work benefits your family, rather than some corporate headquarters is hugely rewarding. Knowing that you are family adds security. If not a safety net, at least some benefit of the doubt. Even if you are the third cousin of the president by his second marriage, working as a file clerk, you can be assured that conflict resolution will be easier for you than the outsider working next to you.

Ask yourself: Can I work with my family 360 days a year and enjoy holiday dinners the other five? Will they listen to me at work? Will they accept my ideas for change? Have I spent enough time away from my family to know that I am my own person?

CAN YOU BE A GOOD LISTENER?

Just as your family members need to listen to your ideas, you need to be a good listener. Seriously ask yourself if you are willing to listen and learn for months. You can't just jump in and be the company's star performer, the boss or the crown prince or princess. Even if you are absolutely sure that the business is very old fashioned, take some time to check things out. It is a sure thing that your fresher education, your experience and your talent will help the company. But, jumping right in with all your great thoughts will only cause a backlash of defensiveness.

Listen, understand fully, digest what you've learned. Then, begin with some suggestions. Know that the elder generation, in spite of all its obvious faults and frailties, has a lot to teach you about this specific business that you'll never learn in school or in another business. They've been at it for a long time. Sometimes their best advice will appear to be no advice at all. That sounds like a bad puzzle, but here are three true stories of business founders giving advice on selling a product.

- "Here's an order book. Hit the road and don't come back until it is full."
- "Here's the book *The Secrets of Selling our Product*." (But when you open it up, all the pages are empty.)
- "Remember to take your price list. Go into the lobby during the convention, sit there and read the newspaper."

Whoa, that is not exactly the hard-core marketing advice we've been paying for at seminars. But, take a closer look at the advice these founders are giving:

1. Be diligent
2. Create your own sales style
3. Be present

What great advice! Work hard, be imaginative, show up at work every day. Those are great answers. They allow you the freedom to be yourself. They don't tie you down to the old ways or to memorizing a sales pitch.

The moral of this story is to catch a company elder while he is in a pensive mood and ask him advice. If it seems stupid at first, it may just be the best advice you'll ever get.

BEFORE YOU JOIN ANY FAMILY BUSINESS

Before you sign up for the family firm, follow the check list of tasks below. It is important to be both cautious and thorough before joining any operation, rather than blindly jumping at an opportunity. By asking questions and considering all sides of the issue, you can help protect both your interests and your family relationships.

Following this process has the added benefit of getting to know your family in a different way. You'll start to see them as they are at work, and they may act entirely differently there. Do they seem wiser to you than they did before? The way they act and talk may help you to make your decision. Do they have a lot of wise advice? If so, that is the kind of person you'll want to work around.

1. **Consider the industry as a whole.** Does a family firm of this size have an opportunity to succeed? Ask management about their strategy. Do you like the product or service provided by the business?

2. **Examine the management of the firm.** Do you buy into the mission statement? How quickly will you be able to change that mission state-

ment? Will you be given the opportunity to grow? What is your possible career track? When are members of the elder generation going to step aside? Be wary of a vague answer here!

3. **Examine the feel of the family while they work together.** Is loving support present? Do family members treat each other as professionals? You should join the family business if it feels right.

4. **When you are close to joining the company, get something in writing.** Don't go for the "someday this will all be yours" routine if it comes with low salary and no contract. Don't avoid the hard questions. Don't work from some old assumptions, no matter how long Pops has been telling you that you'll join the business some day.

5. **Discuss termination.** Who can fire you and why? What kind of support can the company give you between jobs? It doesn't hurt to ask for a golden parachute. Termination is the worst case scenario, also discuss the best case scenario. "How often will I be evaluated for promotion? What is the evaluation process like?"

6. **Does this company have a retirement plan?** If not, will they begin one immediately? If not, will you be paid enough to begin your own plan? (See also the chapter on family financial advan-

tages.) Does this company have a payroll savings plan, which they will match, so that you can purchase stock? If not, ask them to start one.

7. **Check your assumptions.** Never assume that joining a family business will give you a cushy, high paying job with no responsibilities. If you think you see family members that are not pulling their weight, you are probably wrong. Meaningful, diligent work is what you are going to get in a family business. If you are looking for a salary without work, a wise board of directors will cut you out of the herd like a sick heifer.

*"A business that
makes nothing but money
is a poor kind of business."*
— Henry Ford

CHAPTER THREE

Hiring Family Members

If you currently have a business that employs *no* family members, you do want to pause and think it through before hiring any. At this point, there are no rules. You never promised anyone in the family a job there, right?

Keeping family and business separate in order to maintain good relationships is an argument that is often made. I have a friend who prohibited his children from ever entering his business. Since this was always made clear, they are a very happy and successful family. My wife of 30 years has rebuffed any offer to work in the business. While I think that we could avoid any conflicts, we've decided to avoid that risk.

The same pause should be taken if you are thinking about making the first big family promotion, or considering the addition of an in-law or other family member. And the big pause should also come when it is time to train your possible successor. If no family member is ready and qualified, hiring an outsider is always an option.

On the other hand, one normally spends about 20 years as a child in the home with parents, brothers and sisters. Consider how relationships can grow and improve when you work with your family for another 40 years. Relationships mature and mellow, they get better. Working together is an opportunity to build great relationships.

While taking your pause, think about the maturity of the family member that you might hire. Will she be able to act like a coworker instead of a niece? Will the nephew continue to grow emotionally and intellectually? When the time comes, will the son stop acting like a son and find himself? If not, perhaps a strictly "business" business is for you. Just because millions have chosen this path doesn't mean that you should.

ADVANTAGE: TRAINING FROM BIRTH

Take advantage of the fact that you have been training the kids from early on — what they can expect and not expect. You have lead by example. You shared your successes and failures with family members at the dinner table. You don't drive a luxury car unless you expect everyone to be able to drive one. You have taught your children about *entitlement* and *stewardship*. If you haven't, it isn't too late to start.

Entitlement is an interesting word. It comes from the giving of a title such as baron or prince due to birth. Pick a lucky name in the sperm lottery and you are set up for life.

Many family business names have become the icons in their industry: DuPont, Ford, DeBeers,

Rothschild . . . you get the idea. Let's look at a fictional family named Stone.

Founded in 1820 by silversmith Cornelius Stone, the business has thrived for generations, right up to the present. While the stock is publicly traded, 51% is owned by various family members. The company enjoys profits from a large market share of flatware, silver bowls, and candelabras. The present Stone family consists of brothers John and Theodore, and their four adult children. Each of the six live in expensive homes in an upscale suburb of Boston. They all have income in the mid-six figure range from salary and dividends. Does this mean that the grand-children, the seventh generation from Cornelius Stone, will be born with the ultimate silver spoons in their mouths? That they will be crowned the queen or king of silver?

Perhaps. But everything depends upon family culture. Let's say the family has an annual forum at which the matriarch or patriarch addresses the teenagers in this way: "Through diligence, cleverness and a lot of good fortune, your ancestors have provided this family with a comfortable lifestyle. Each of the members of the fifth and sixth generation have also worked and have earned their own way. You are expected to do the same. While we have become accustomed to a nice lifestyle, it is because we have worked for it, not because we are entitled to it. We will avoid conspicuous consumption. Let's work to bring honor to the family and business that bear our name. Family members have rights but they also have responsibilities. We believe that all family members should be afforded an appropriate education. They will be loved and nurtured. As you become adults, you are free to apply for work in the business, if qualified, or free to seek employment elsewhere."

Such a story, repeated often, surely will build an understanding. The adults will have to be great examples. Perhaps a really rigid family like this will go so far as to have an inner disciplinary committee to rein in those who start jet setting around, who lead a playboy or playgirl lifestyle. Then a strong culture of work first, profit sharing later, is established.

Let's come back to earth. Not everyone is born into a family like this. Perhaps you are the granddaughter of the founders of a small grocery store. This store today is struggling. To what are you entitled?

In my opinion you are entitled to exactly the same thing: the right to work and the right to love.

In addition to training your children about entitlement and conspicuous consumption, there are other ways to teach them the positive side of business.

When you come home from work, share the positive points of the day. You got an unexpected order, that made you feel confident. An employee made a surprising gain in ability. You negotiated a better contract with a supplier. Anything as long as it is upbeat.

Not only did I work at menial jobs as a youngster, my dad sent me to Mexico and France to learn the languages. He knew the company was expanding internationally and he wanted someone with language skills. So from age 12 we studied Spanish together, then off I went at age 14 to study abroad. This was great training for any vocation, and great training for life.

In my parents' home international visitors were brought home for dinner. My wife and I continue this tradition. Making customers into friends is easy while dining in your home, it is good business and it makes business pleasurable. Furthermore it teaches your children that the business can be fun.

ADVANTAGE: FAMILY LOYALTY

The flip side of any negativity associated with entitlement is the fact that you are careful with your product when it carries your name. When you have grown up with your name on a building, you care about that building. Imagine how great it would be to grow up seeing your name on dozens of trucks or on products that benefit people. Youngsters who go through this make sure to prepare themselves, so that they can bring honor to the business. Take advantage of this. How? By hiring them!

You may want to consider whether employment at your business would prevent your children from doing something different. If you would prefer them to choose other professions instead of doing what you do, lovingly guide them in the direction of your mutual dreams. If your plan is to sell your business to fund your retirement, that is perfectly fine. It is just best to let your family know that as early as possible.

Consider that once you do hire the first family member, it will be expected that you will hire more. The rest of the family will make that assumption, perhaps even make the assumption that your business is their safety net. They reason that they can take on another job, and if they can't make it, it's no big deal. "I'll go into the family business as a last resort." Therefore it is important that from the very beginning you do two things:

1. Write a company policy on the hiring of family
2. Let everyone in the family know about it
   (See sample on next page.)

Consider that hiring family members can be a huge advantage for your business. At the start up stage, your children are cheap, part time, loyal employees. During the expansion phase, young family members have the energy and ability to help your company to grow. Before the maturity phase, family members are needed for reinvention and diversification.

Celebrate and take advantage of their differences. Johnny is good at vehicle maintenance, Sally loves keeping the books, and Mom is a natural sales person. Consider that your big competitors are hiring clones of themselves, while you have the oppor-

TOOL BOX:

Sample Nepotism Policy

- Family members must meet the same criteria for hiring as non-family applicants.

- Family members are expected to meet the same performance level required of non-family members.

- As a general principle, family members will be supervised by non-family members.

- Family members may not be hired by their closest relative.

- Family members may be offered a 12 month internship by the board of directors. Then a committee of three will make a recommendation to the Board whether or not to offer full time employment. A second 12 month internship might be advisable. Compensation will be at fair market value for the position held.

- Family members are encouraged to get work experience outside the company before applying. Their work experience will be a guiding factor in the decision whether to hire.

tunity to choose creative winners that are family members that you trust. You have the opportunity to bring love into your workplace, and that is a good thing as well.

ADVANTAGE: OUTSIDE EXPERIENCE

I was approached by the son of a very good customer. His father was putting pressure on him to get a job, specifically with him. The son had just finished college. The son appealed to me to talk to his father, to encourage him to allow the son to get outside experience. So I pulled down the texts from my bookshelf and studied up. The academics were unanimous. Their answer is that the son/daughter/next generation member should get outside experience for two to eight years.

- The youngsters need to make the choice of joining the business themselves. Without this freedom of choice, they won't perform to peak level.

- The youngsters need to work for someone that isn't a parent. This is in order to learn the difference between a parent and a boss.

- This break in time gives the parent a chance to quit parenting. When the youngsters join, they are treated like adult employees, not like parented children.

- The youngsters should work outside to learn how to make decisions, to learn how to take responsibility for their own actions. If not, it will be too easy to say "Maybe I made a mistake, but it was my parents' fault".

- Working for a company that is larger than yours prepares them for the added complexity that your business will have with its own growth.

- They can learn management systems and practices unknown inside the family firm.

- They will meet and make connections with people that can help later.

- They can help to identify new markets, different types of competitors, and different strategies.

- They will learn to fly or fall without the family safety net.

- They will build self esteem

- They will learn to face the traumas of transfer, promotion, termination and competition.

- Non-family employees will respect that the young hires have earned their way into the business with outside experience, not just *blood equity*.

- They will learn their true market value of salary and benefits.

- They will learn for themselves if the outside world is better.

- Parents aren't really ready to give up any of the decision making until they are about 60 years old.

Wow, that is some list! It seems to me that I'd better backtrack 30 years and start over again. I skipped my college graduation ceremony, so that I could start in the family business more quickly. I was happy with the offered salary — $1,000 a month was pretty good in 1974. And the plan was for me to start our California branch, so I wasn't going to be under my dad's thumb anyway.

The experts are unanimous:
Members of the next generation should
get outside work experience
before coming to work in the family firm.

As you probably guessed, it didn't start out too well. Instead of my dad staying in California for a week at the start, he moved in with me. Instead of me being the branch manager, I was one of his grunt laborers. After a couple of months pouring concrete and installing equipment, I suggested that it was time for him to hit the highway, to really let me be in charge. He replied "But you don't know how to do anything." Hmmm, calculating his age at the time, he was 58. He needed two more years before he was ready to trust me, and in retrospect, I needed a couple years experience under a boss that wasn't my dad. But you know what? We broke the rule and got along fine in the long run.

From my current perspective, I am pleased with the fresh education and experience when we hire new young people. They bring us something that our relatively closed system did not have.

My own son Cody is now getting his outside experience. We do believe the academics are correct. Perhaps he'll find another career and never enter our business, we'll just have to take that risk. If he does not join us, that is fine with me as long as he's happy. My customer's son? He went to work in the family business.

ADVANTAGE: A SHARED DREAM

Do the important family members in your company have a Shared Dream? Does each want the same thing from the company?

A good friend called me with questions about bringing his son into his business. The son was qualified, and the situations of the 67-year-old father and 40-year-old son seemed to mesh nicely. The question wasn't whether to hire the son, but what to do next to insure that it was "done right".

My advice was for the father to write down his dream for the future of the company as it existed *before* the son came back into the picture. I knew he had been trying to sell the company. If the son joined the business, it could continue or it still could be sold.

I suggested that the son should also write down his dream for the company, then the two should compare their notes, their vision of where the company should go. Are the two dreams the same, or at least compatible?

During this process one needs to separate emotions from logic. To discuss money in a frank, businesslike way. Then if there is family baggage involved, open up that luggage and have an emotional laundry day. Clearing the air of grievances might be temporarily painful, but it opens the door to a peaceful new start.

While a Shared Dream can include dreamy elements, when looking at succession, it should also include:

- an exit strategy
- a strategy for how profits should be used
- a date for change of leadership.

These are vital questions in any family business during succession. They are important at any time, because it is never too early to be thinking about succession.

Exit Strategy. All parties need to be aware that the business founder needs to finance his retirement. He built the company and has a dream of a certain lifestyle when he departs. Where will the money come from?

Profit Strategy. Will the company be a cash cow, to be milked for the good of the founder? Or for the good of the son, who may have some immediate needs? Or will profit be rolled back into the company for expansion or debt reduction?

A Date. One of the most common complaints of next generation family business members is that "dad" just won't go away. He's not paying attention to daily matters, his key accounts have been replaced with better ones, he isn't up to date on technology. But he is still present. This presence is helpful at times in different ways.

It is important to avoid a "gift of the magi" situation. For example, the son may decide to keep some important strategy the way dad would do it. Or the way he *thinks* dad would do it. But, dad really wants the son to take the company in whatever direction will lead to success in today's world. Neither is really in charge, both are relying on the other for leadership. Each gives the other the gift of leadership, but neither one takes it.

The answer is to set a date. Whether the agreement is a contract written by an attorney or an informal memo is up to you. Have it in writing that the elder will absolutely be done with ownership, management and leadership by a certain date, or dates.

Remember when examining a Shared Dream that every family member, regardless of age, gender, employment in the company, or ownership has a stake in the business and deserves to be heard.

Ignoring anyone can lead to problems. You want your business and your family to be mutually supportive, to capitalize on each other's strengths, and to be more successful together than either could be alone.

Make sure that all of the family members in your company have a Shared Dream.

As you examine hiring family members, I will admit that there are "complications" when working at a business with family. But for me personally, after three decades of plenty of those, I can honestly say that I would do it again. My family and I have learned to recognize the tough situations and to deal with them. We take the emotional part of the problem aside and examine it. We examine the business options, and then find accord between them. While doing so, we appreciate that we are doing the hard thing. Doing the hard thing is what allows a family business to survive into the next generation.

"*Success is not
the key to happiness.
Happiness is the key to success.
If you love what you are doing,
you will be successful.*"
— Albert Schweitzer

CHAPTER FOUR

Having Fun at Work
with the Family

I f you've worked with your parents, children or siblings, you know that there will be disagreements.
Family members quarrel; they have feuds. They get sulky.
Businesses have been split or shredded because family
members couldn't tolerate each other. How can family
members get along at work?

The answer is simple: Being a nice person goes a long
way towards family unity. How many of these things do *you*
do with family members that you work with?

- Cheerfully say "Hello" when you meet, let them know
  you are happy to see them
- Send their children a birthday card
- Compliment them on their work
- Offer personal help in time of stress, need, sickness
- Ask them for help
- Do something special for the whole family
- Sincerely inquire about them and their inner family
- Let them win an argument

- Admit you were wrong
- Say "I respect you" "I love you" "I understand you"

If you have a reputation around the job as a taskmaster or a loner, try working some of the ideas above. They are tools that work. The emotional benefit of doing something nice lubricates all the other interactions. Instead of someone getting down on you for an error, they will go easier.

A HAPPIER BUSINESS ENVIRONMENT

Communication is the key to a harmonious business environment, but many people confuse communication with talking. Communication includes talking, listening *and* responding. Responding in a work environment, especially one infused with family members, can be tricky.

A concept called "Response-Ability" (coined in the book *Top 20 Teens* that details a school curriculum for Thinking, Learning and Communicating or TLC) is one of the best things I have heard on the subject. Response-Ability is simply the ability to respond to negative input in a positive, mature way.

Here is one example of Response-Ability: A family member abruptly says, "You shouldn't be working on the that project! It is below you and you are needed on more important things." You, on the other hand, believe in the particular project and feel it deserves your work. Instead of an immediate angry reaction, you simply say, "OK. Thanks," and then sleep on it. You take the time to decide on a better response such as: "May we discuss the project that you took me off of yesterday? I think that the project can be turned over to someone else soon, but I feel that it does deserve my time now because no one else here knows the details like me. My goal is that it will not stay a small project, that it will be a real money maker for us."

While you may be boiling mad or feeling hurt by a family member's comment, you still have the ability to respond in a responsible, positive way — a way that will not escalate tension or disagreement. Also remember that the mature person *forgets* about such incidents, so that there is no lingering hidden agenda later.

Avoid thinking to yourself: "This family member is really a problem." Individuals are not problems, they are sensitive, thinking humans with the ability to learn. When you have a problem, think of it as being a *thing* that is between you and that family member. Examine the problem, not the person. Even examine this floating problem with that person, because their point of view may be very informative. The two of you may even be able to collaborate on a solution to the problem.

Spell everything out. It is important for everyone to work *on* the business, as well as to work *in* the business. It is essential to write job descriptions and update them regularly. Family members are lucky that they have quick understanding of each other, not to mention love. But families in business should not avoid the good business of written job descriptions. The more frequently and casually you discuss guidelines, expectations, roles and perspectives the better you will feel about your working relationships.

IT IS VITAL TO TAKE TIME
TO EMPTY THE FAMILY BAGGAGE.

Empty the family baggage. Because you are working with family members, it is sometimes vital to have a meeting solely designed to empty the family baggage. Such a meeting might take a few minutes, or it might take a weekend retreat with a family advisor. Are you afraid that there will be unpleasantness in such a meeting? *Of course* there will be unpleasantness, we are talking about a family business here. And if you are afraid, that indicates that something needs to be done in this area. It is better to have a frequent series of small conflicts than to have one big blowup. Face your fear or your uneasiness because it never is as bad as you anticipate. Start today. Establish a feeling of calm before Christmas so that no one says "OK then, you're fired. Please pass the roast beef."

Throughout this process, remind yourself that what you do benefits your family and your business. Doing the hard stuff right is what will make you successful. Work on your own attitude first. Like removing a band-aid, realize that it will soon be over, it will soon be healed. One quick yank is better than a slow process.

Jump right into it. Don't send a memo announcing that a meeting will be held in three months. Simply make a list of leading questions: "How is the business looking from your point of view lately?" "Do you have some ideas for possible changes to your job description?" "Have I interfered with your responsibilities lately?"

Once you have your list, find a neutral area for your casual meeting. This is a "hats-off" meeting, and no one likes to talk to someone sitting behind a desk. Find a place without a phone, and turn off the cell phones.

If family baggage does comes up (You've never trusted me!), it is important to acknowledge the other's feelings. Do not deny feelings, everyone is entitled to them. But once feelings are acknowledged and heard, return to the business at hand and treat it in a businesslike way.

Take Advantage of a Safety Net

When the family and the business rub up against each other, it can often create friction or something I like to simply call "The Hard Stuff." Emptying the family baggage, like explained above, is a great example of dealing with The Hard Stuff in the right way. While it can make you squeamish and uncomfortable to deal with The Hard Stuff, think of it as establishing a safety net under your tightrope. Life has upsets, and family upsets affect your business. Such things as divorces, personal bankruptcies, and mental illness are big distractions.

Dealing with The Hard Stuff in the right way will help you establish a safety net.

If you've managed The Hard Stuff in the right way, you will be cushioned by your safety net of friends, family and coworkers. You will have support and help from the diverse personalities, so that the crisis passes. Then, you get back to having fun with your family at work.

CHALLENGE THE WAY
IT HAS ALWAYS BEEN DONE

Let's face it; doing the same thing over and over is not fun. Especially, if you are doing the same old thing the way your grandparents did it. Have fun by inventing a better way of doing it. As a 12-year-old child, my friend Bill and I helped another friend assemble hot dog boxes at his dad's meat processing plant. We invented ways to do the chore faster, so we could go out and play faster.

Let's move up several notches from assembling cardboard boxes. Let's say your grandfather has a decades-old policy against exporting your product. Take a stab at presenting him with the idea of breaking this unbreakable rule. If you bump into resistance, consider it as a challenge. While you may be telling Grandpa that it is time for new ideas, it is good to remember this bit of wisdom from my old childhood pal Bill: "You can say anything to anyone as long as you have a smile on your face." Don't let unbreakable rules break your spirit. Think like an owner, even if you are not an owner. Doing so is not only fun, but it is good for business.

TOO MANY COOKS SPOIL THE BROTH

Let's examine the truism "Too many cooks spoil the broth." If you have six family members in the kitchen and each one adds his favorite ingredient, perhaps the broth will in fact be spoiled. Ingredients as diverse as tarragon, shrimp, pasta, strawberries, molasses and chile probably won't work. But that concoction would be the result of poor communication rather than having too many cooks.

Brainstorming is a good business technique to initiate creativity. The more people you have in the brainstorming session the better. Similarly, the more input from family members about the business the better.

Founders have a reputation of liking to work alone. Don't let this attitude carry on for generations. The more ideas that come from the younger generation, the quicker your business will adapt to the changing world. When you have an atmosphere of fun and cooperation, your business will stay young and healthy. Allowing the younger family members the freedom to be creative, even when they make some mistakes, prepares them as future leaders.

HAVE FUN BY HAVING FUN

Sometimes you ought to have some corporate fun. One October our entire staff went to the parking lot with small pumpkins. We set up our product, tin cans full of seed, as bowling pins. We all bowled across the macadam with pumpkins, and had lots of laughs. The normal differences between supervisors and workers dissolved for a while.

Every month we have "First Friday Club," which is an hour long staff meeting. Everyone is expected to attend. Not only do we share information among the different departments, but we have some laughs.

Every Christmas we buy inexpensive gifts and play "Dirty Santa," a game where you draw numbers for the gifts and steal them from each other. Games like this have the ability to wash away the minor resentments that build up in any workplace.

Some firms go so far as to assign a C.F.O., a Chief Fun Officer, who has a budget and the extra job of planning company fun.

"Feelings of worth can flourish
only in an atmosphere where
individual differences are appreciated,
mistakes are tolerated,
communication is open,
and rules are flexible —
the kind of atmosphere
that is found in a nurturing family."

— Virginia Satir

CHAPTER FIVE

Communicating with Family

You've heard of identical twins that know what the other is thinking. One completes the sentence before the first one can. I believe all family members have some *intuitive communication.*

Meeting in the hallway at work, Janet and her mom exchange a few words. Also communicated are volumes that outsiders don't understand. One's body language before the conversation even begins communicates something. The rolling of eyes, a shrug or hand gesture saves words. A reference to a team member that is "just like old Pete Ahlers" conjures up memories. More has been communicated in 30 seconds than might be exchanged between people from different backgrounds in 15 minutes. In this way, family businesses can be more efficient than others.

Take advantage of intuitive communication by making decisions quickly. Once you have the understanding among the decision makers, make the decision. You've just gained a week on your bureaucratic competitor! They are having meetings; they are still talking about it.

People from the same family tend to think alike. They have the same culture. They have the same stories, going back generations. Perhaps without even knowing it, the older generation has given valuable lessons simply by talking about work at home. A mission statement or the "strategic vision" are not needed by a close family: they live them. The vision is shared, as if by osmosis.

Family members who work together
have the benefit of intuitive communication.

Take advantage of really knowing your family members by choosing when *not* to talk. You planned to have a technical discussion with your sister at 10:00 am. One chat in the morning, and you know that this isn't the right day. Be sensitive to the moods of all your family members. Choose the right time to discuss the difficult topics.

Build on the communication advantage by getting even better at it. Improve your active listening skills. Keep your eyes on the speaker. Be quiet. Maintain receptive body language. Repeat back what you think you've heard. Learn what it feels like to be a good listener and practice.

GETTING ALONG

"Getting along" isn't the same as communication. Just because your relationship is temporarily unpleasant, it doesn't mean that you aren't communicating. It means there was a problem. When any two family members are getting on each other's nerves, there is always a solution. Try these mind adjustments or activities:

- Realize that there exists a problem which is *separate* from you and the other person.
- Take a breather, allow the feelings from any disagreement to calm down.
- Realize that it is easier to change yourself, than to change the other person.
- Fight the urge to dislike the person, even just a little.
- Don't be defensive, instead give the other person a chance.
- Compliment the other person (even if you have to look really hard!).
- Show RESPECT for the other person.
- Let the other person make a decision or win another debate.
- Do something fun with the other person: Throw a Frisbee. Watch a football game. Take everyone to a movie and dinner.

Try the above items. Let some time pass. Try them again. Work on your own feelings, that is the only thing that you can really control. After some time, the problem will be gone.

Always remember the number one rule of getting along: It's easier to change yourself than to fix the other person.

Let's look at two fictional conversations:

JERRY: Dad, you hurt my feelings all the time, you need to learn to respect my feelings more.

DAD: No one can give you respect, you have to earn it.

JERRY: You've been watching too many re-runs of *Dallas*. You have no clue how to get along with people, and you treat family worse than other staff.

DAD: Who are you to be telling me anything? You are not above being fired, so you better stop criticizing me.

OK, maybe that was a bit brutal even for our families. This wasn't a conversation, it was a battle. Let's try that conversation over again, where both are trying to be more positive.

JERRY: We have had our little problems, and I am going to work on myself to avoid them in the future. Just like we all got along well in the ballpark yesterday, I want us all to get on well here at work.

DAD: We did have fun at the game yesterday. But do you just want to have fun at work all the time?

JERRY: No. But, staying on task at work doesn't mean *never* having fun. What we really need is better communication among us family members here at work. In order to improve, we need to have some give and take, and we need a lot of respect for each other. We need to treat each other as professionals, and I've probably been the worst at that.

DAD: If you want to have better communication here, I'll help. I do think you are a professional. I'll be ready to listen to your other ideas.

JERRY: Maybe we could even formalize our better communication by creating a code of conduct for the family.

This time, Dad's remark "But do you just want to have fun at work all the time?" was not taken defensively. It was not treated as a sword thrust that must be parried. Jerry didn't get pulled into an argument.

Dad did a good job of active listening here. He repeated back what he thought he heard Jerry say. Dad wasn't jabbing, and Jerry didn't make the mistake of telling Dad to improve himself. In my experience, telling the other person to improve himself never works. See sample Code of Conduct on the next page.

TOOL BOX:

Sample Code of Conduct

A Code of Conduct is a set of rules for family members that are working together. It might include such items as:

- We will support each other in front of other employees.
- We will not judge each other.
- We will not take any assets out of the business except as salary and formal benefits, these benefits to be determined by the board of directors.
- We will publicly recognize the accomplishments of each family employee.
- We will maintain family and work boundaries, avoiding discussion of business at family functions.

BUILD ON FAMILY TRUST

Good communication is based on trust. If you don't trust someone to tell you the truth, you won't take what you hear from him at face value. Use the simple test on the next page to identify any trust deficiencies in your family business.

TRUST GUT TEST

DIRECTIONS: Make a list of family members that are working in your family business, or who are passive owners. Next to each one, write down whether you trust them. Have separate columns for some different questions:

Name	#1	#2	#3	#4	#5
Pete					
Sally					
Uncle Joe					
Bernard					

QUESTIONS:

#1: If I leave {insert family member name here} $100,000 cash on Friday, do I trust him/her to have it all when I need it back on Monday?

 # 2: Do I trust {insert family member name here} to uphold the welfare of the business before he/she upholds his/her personal welfare?

 # 3: Do I trust {insert family member name here} to get a job done without me having to go back and double check on him/her? (Or, if he/she is your supervisor: "Do I trust him/her to give me clear instructions and a fair evaluation?")

 # 4: Do I trust {insert family member name here} to do his/her job correctly?

 # 5: Do I trust {insert family member name here} to behave in a predictable manner?

Now expand your list of people to include several coworkers that are not family members. How do the results compare?

You will most likely find that your family members all receive a check under "behave in a predictable manner." On the other hand, non-family coworkers may be more likely to act in an unpredictable manner. You don't know them as well, and you don't trust them as much because they have different backgrounds and values.

This "Trust Gut Test" will either highlight trust deficiencies in your family business or hopefully demonstrate the intuitive trust you have when working with family members.

COMMUNICATE WITH NON-FAMILY AS IF THEY ARE FAMILY

It is as important to be upfront with non-family coworkers as it is family members. For example, when our management team was first into the process of recruiting my son-in-law, we went to the entire staff. At our monthly meeting, my management team and I said, "We have been talking to Larry's son-in-law about the possibility of working at Hollar Seeds. We are aware of the positive and negative aspects of hiring him as opposed to hiring a non-family member. He doesn't have experience in this industry, but he has a reason to live in this area — to be near his family. This would be an arms-length agreement; we are not giving him a position because he is family. Here are his qualifications. We'll be talking to all of you about your opinion on this topic. Many of you will have the chance to interview him, and to give your frank opinion about him back to us."

In our case, 100% of staff welcomed the idea. If they had not, we would have dealt with that, and perhaps not made the job offer. In effect, we made family members of the whole staff by sharing the family decision with them. And, we handled a business decision in a businesslike way. This was juggling at its best.

There are also likely scenarios where you give a family member without qualifications a job to help him or her out. If you know the common wisdom against this practice and choose to break the rule, that is fine with me — family first. But, talk to your non-family staff about it. It isn't fair to the new hire to say "Ronnie is as dumb as a bag of hammers," but it is appropriate to be straight with the person's supervisor. You might say, "Perhaps Ronnie isn't the best person for this position right now, but I believe that he has potential and is about to turn the corner. Please help me, the business and the family out by doing your best with him. Teach him, push him, and supervise him like a non-family member. Give him warnings if needed, and apply the same company policy on termination to him as you would anyone, should it come to that."

FAMILY TERMINATIONS ARE EASY

He knows it is coming. You've warned him, trained him, and given him expectations. He isn't meeting the goals that you both agreed to. Don't worry about this decision.

Terminations of family members are easy because you know where he is going afterwards. He is going back home, where he has a nurturing family. Terminations of outsiders are more difficult because you worry about what will happen to them afterwards. Make a plan, perhaps consulting with the emotional leader of the family about how to show respect for the one that is being fired.

You are definitely walking the fine line between business and family when you fire a family member. When you talk to him or her, it is important to remember that. You might say: "Having only the business in my mind right now, I have to say that your employment here did not work out as planned. I'm giving you notice of your termination. Now, as one of your family members, let me say that the family is going to support you 100% while you look for a position that will make you happy. Would you like to go back to school? Whatever passion you have in life, let's work together so that your dreams will come true." During the entire process, remind yourself of these three things:

- *That person fired himself through his performance*
- *Keeping a poor performer is bad for staff morale*
- *No one was ever fired too quickly*

EMOTIONAL LEADER

Your family firm may have two leaders, and you don't even know it. One is steering the business, the other is guiding the family. The second is the Emotional Leader, the "go-to" person when anyone in the family has a personal problem.

It could be that your business leader is also the Emotional Leader. If this is you, you are juggling constantly and need to know which ball is in your hand at all times. Are you being approached on a personal, emotional issue? If so, you should treat it with heart, rather than with business logic.

Emotional Leaders may talk to the family about entitlement, as discussed in Chapter Three. Emotional Leaders will often have his or her finger on the pulse of the family in a better way than the business leader. These two should work together to juggle the needs of the family and of the business.

If you are the Emotional Leader, realize that you will be approached with complaints and gossip.

You'll be approached with "He said/She said." The wise emotional leader will not allow this to go into *triangulation.* He should counsel the person to take his problem directly to the source of the problem and work it out directly. It is also important that the Emotional Leader never speak ill of anyone that is not present. If he did, no one would trust him as Emotional Leader. (Would you?) Sometimes the best communication technique is just keeping your mouth shut.

If your Emotional Leader is outside the business, she may have a different perspective. She may be better at seeing when the family dynamic is interfering with logical business decisions, or when strict business logic is interfering with family. The family's Emotional Leader often has the emotional intelligence to bring the different branches of the family into accord. Spouses of business people can be powerful consultants and allies. They have absorbed business information for years, and they likely know you better than anyone else. Often they can communicate something to you that no one else can.

DELEGATION

A friend was struggling with a growing business. He couldn't do everything himself and was having a hard time trusting his staff. They had several big landscaping projects going at once, one of which was reaching an important deadline, but they had a problem with a giant boulder. "I was busy, so I just told the foreman that he had two days to finish the job any way he could and to finish it right," the owner said. "The next thing I knew, the foreman had rented this gigantic crane at such a big expense that we lost money on the project. He met the deadline and the quality, but not the budget."

Proper delegation requires a lot of communication, so in general family businesses are better at it than others. Build on that strength by knowing how to delegate and by balancing between the two extremes. The first extreme is to micro-manage. You define the project's desirable outcomes, explain its importance, assign responsibility, explain exactly how to do everything, check up on progress frequently and have an evaluation process . . . and then take credit for everything. The second extreme is to wash your hands. For example, you might say, "Hey, Joe, answer my e-mails for a week while I'm gone. Bye."

My friend, with the landscape business, was in no position to criticize his foreman if the budget had not been explained. The person who is delegating work needs to make the important points clear from the outset. The details depend on the experience of the person getting the new task. In general, it is better for family members in upper management to stay away from the project site, rather than to be checking up too often. There are two reasons for this. First, inspections by the boss make the statement: "I don't trust the new supervisor." Second, you might be tempted to tell him how to do it your way, and you may happily discover that the person you have delegated to has an even better way. Don't get mad about that, it is *good* news.

The person getting the new job can help as well. From the beginning, she should ask questions in any area where she has concerns. What is the budget? When do you expect this to be done? What authority do I have? Will I be evaluated at the end of the project, or will there be surprise inspections?

Some people want and need more coaching, others want free reign. Hire qualified family members, then communicate well. Be prepared to spend much more time on training than it would take for you to do the job yourself. That time will come back to you when the job is done by someone else in the future.

Businesses need to be renewed.
Families are the
natural renewal system.

CHAPTER SIX

Taking Advantage of Change

My customers say, "We don't like your new melon; it's not right for our market. People in this country are slow to accept change. Farmers want to plant what they've always been planting. Don't even change that old picture on the label; even if you have a better one, we are used to the old one."

I've heard all the excuses. What they are really saying is: I don't want to WORK for change. I'm resentful of this attitude for a very good reason — change is where the money is. Not just for my company, but for our customers and their customers as well.

For decades there was no change in the kind of squash used in the Middle East. Many suppliers had small shares of the market with a cheap commodity product. It was a white marrow type squash. In 1969, I sent samples of our hybrid to several countries. It increased yield by 50% but the color was light green instead of white.

My customers were critical of the idea that I would suggest such a change. "Larry, Larry, Larry. You have to understand. We want the white squash, not light green squash." I heard this story from customers in Jordan, Lebanon, and Syria. Two years later Petoseed introduced Clarita, which was nearly the same as ours. Clarita became the best selling squash of all time, capturing an astounding-ly large percent of the market. It laid the groundwork for fol-low up varieties and gave their brand momentum to introduce other novel products.

Years later, I was visiting a customer in Amman. He reverently showed me the tiny garden in his park-ing lot where he discovered Clarita. Not only did he grow the plants, but unlike my cus-tomers that grew my plants,

KNOW THAT LIGHT BULB EVENTS CAN BE GOOD FOR BUSINESS.

a light bulb went on. He realized he could introduce something that was different. This light bulb event made him rich.

What are the necessary steps in acceptance of change?

- An open mind, and curiosity
- A light bulb event
- Willingness to work, to work for change
- A marketing test
- Work and persistence

Change requires work. But when the world changes from the standard product to your product, it will be worth it.

Perhaps there is resistance to change within your organization due to family dynamics. People from different generations need to listen to each other. They need to listen, and then have an open mind and a willingness to test something new. If your company has one dominating older person that listens to no one, you are not alone. There is something about the personality of founders, of the entrepreneurial generation, that leads them to be poor listeners. They can be obstinate know-it-alls. The next generation has these options:

- **Work somewhere else.** Not a bad idea, at least until The Old One sets a retirement date.
- **Put up with them passively.** You can safely do this while learning all of the good stuff that The Old One knows, but beware. Sometimes founders are still on the job at age 95. You may

want to retire before they do, never having been the boss or inventor yourself.

- **Fight them, push, cajole, gain power.** This option depends on your two personalities, but this is my preferred answer. Here you are juggling your position within the company with that of The Old One. Juggle on!

CHANGE IS GOOD FOR BUSINESS

Ringo Starr's song "It Don't Come Easy" applies perfectly to succession with lyrics like: "I don't want much, I only want trust." Imagine these words spoken by the younger generation, to which the elder replies "but you know it don't come easy." It takes a lot of time and patience.

One roadblock to change is that the younger generation and the older generation are so much alike. Did that suggestion sound absurd? If you object to any hint that you are like your parent, then you *are* like him. You can't help but be like him, he's been an example to you your whole life. The nut doesn't fall far from the tree. It's great to have him as an example for 18 or 20 years. It's great to have him as an example for 50 years. But sooner or later, you will *become* him to a large degree, which is good and bad for your family business. First of all, it maintains the status quo that your staff and customers got used to. And, The Old One will be more comfortable with you at the helm than someone else. However, if you are too much like your elder, you will miss one great advantage of a family business — Businesses need to be renewed. Families are a natural renewal system.

In order to take advantage of change, you need to grow as an individual so that your work renews your family firm. Imagine that your business is this sailing ship. Some people are the sails. They push the organization. Others are workers that lower the sails, and then pull the oars. The boss decides which direction the boat is going, but anyone can come up with an idea for change. The new kid can say: "Let's build a taller mast" or "Let's veer a little bit in that direction."

Not every suggestion from the youngster will be good. But if every new idea is ignored, soon there will be no more new ideas. If your organization is truly stuck at "This is the way we've always done it," you should ask the questions: "And where exactly did that get you? Are you absolutely sure that this business is the best that it could possibly be? And will what worked in the past still work in the future?"

EXAMINE TRUISMS

As members of different generations discuss business options, truisms are sure to be shared by the elder. "Walk more than you talk." "Business comes first, then personal gain." "The customer is always right." "Never buy a piece of equipment that won't pay for itself in three years." When the older person spouts a truism it usually stops the discussion right there.

While it is always good practice to examine truisms , DO NOT let them stop the conversation. Examine carefully this wisdom of the past. Look at all of the what-if scenarios. Ask yourself, "Does this saying still apply to today's world?" Just because a tactic worked at one time, it doesn't mean that it will be the best tactic now.

Examine truisms,
but don't allow them to end the conversation.

Let's look at one example: "Children should be seen, not heard." This was always a conversation stopper in my family. While there may be times and places for this truism, let's look at this from different perspectives:

- Children should always be heard
- Children are encouraged to contribute business ideas
- Due to their naiveté, children are the best opportunity we have to start thinking outside the box

Whenever your "Old One" intones the oft repeated family truism, try examining just the opposite. You won't always trash it, but sometimes you will due to changing circumstances. The important point is to not accept the truism just because it sounds wise and has been around a long time.

However, sometimes truisms are worth saving. For example, a longtime member of the seed industry told me that his dad liked to say, "Never buy something until you know where the money is coming from to pay for it." He and I discussed and examined the truism and decided that it was one that was worth keeping. My friend examined that with me, and decided that it was a good one. "Build with your profit," a favorite of R.H. James, the man my dad bought the business from, sounds out of date in today's world of IPOs. But, in my opinion, it is still powerful wisdom.

If you have a family truism, please send it to me at Larry@fambizjuggler.com. I may want to use it for my next book, so let me know if that is permissible.

IN A NUTSHELL

The younger generation has a fresher education. Take advantage of that! If you are the older generation, listen to their points of view. Borrow their textbooks. Give them a chance to try something. Even if you're sure that the youngster will fail, how can she learn except through experience? And perhaps you are sure that she'll fail because you failed at the same idea 25 years ago. Well, maybe the parameters have changed in 25 years. Take advantage of young ideas.

If you are of the younger generation, just keep having the new ideas and keep testing them. Juggle on!

It's not what you know
but who you know
that makes the difference.

CHAPTER SEVEN

Using Family Firm Connections

A **young friend of mine called** and asked my advice: "My dad gave me this job, now he isn't letting me do it. Did that ever happen to you?" Well, it happened to me and probably to about 14 million other sons of bosses. Yet, my friend felt like he was all alone. He felt like his situation was unique, maybe that it was his fault. But he did exactly the right thing, he checked with someone else who might have had the same problem.

The perfect advice for you, no matter what problem you are facing, is free. You just have to ask the right person. The more connections you have with other family businesses the better your chance of getting that advice. Use the box on the next page to help you create a list of connections you probably already have. If you can't think of many, pull out your high school yearbook and look for old acquaintances. If they are in a family business near you, you'll have a double bond with them — a shared alma mater and a family firm.

TOOL BOX:

Who are your connections?

Spend a little time making a list of people you know. Consider the following: Suppliers, customers, local businesses, a family firm in your industry which has a different product from yours, membership in organizations like The Executive Committee (TEC) or Young President's Organization (YPO), or a relative with a family business.

_____

_____

_____

_____

_____

_____

_____

_____

_____

_____

_____

_____

I love to make new friendships by discussing family business with anyone in family business. It is amazing how much you will learn about them in a hurry. And the friendships created through discussion of family business will improve as you find yourselves helping each other. "How is your leadership transition going?" and similar questions open the door for great conversations.

No matter how long or short your list is, make a point of communicating with some of them. If you want to become connected, if you want to spread your safety net, you need to be active. All it takes is changing from drab small talk to real conversations about family in business.

A great place to look for advice, solace or friendship is from someone in a business like yours who is not a competitor. For example, while our business specializes in the production of watermelon seed, the Christiansons specialized in spinach seed. For two generations we've met them at conventions and discussed questions like: "What percent of sales are you spending on advertising these days?" "What are you doing for seed business specific software?" "Are you close to financing your retirement?" "Let's compare the progress of some mutual customers." These are discussions that you don't want to have with a direct competitor, but would like to have with someone very much like yourself.

Ken Christianson is one of my best pals in the industry. He is a great person to talk to because his business was more complex. His business was bigger, at a size where we hope to be in a few years. He was third generation while I am in the second generation. His family was larger and his ownership was more complex than ours. We're the same age, and I've always gained valuable insights from him.

*Family firm connections
can offer loyal friendships,
mutually-profitable relationships,
great sources of advice and powerful allies
for generations.*

Sometimes I want to talk to older persons. They can be very powerful allies and sources of advice. Our strongest supplier-customer bonds are with family firms that we have known for generations. "You don't have to give me the hard sell, Larry, I'll always buy from Hollar because your dad gave my father credit when no one else would." "Son, meet Larry, his father sold seed to your grandfather, you can trust Hollar Seeds, and they are a family business." Expressions of loyalty like that cannot be purchased with advertising money. Introductions like that have made our work a great pleasure. Elder family members in companies like that are great people to talk to about your problems.

Khalil Miqdadi, founder of Agricultural Materials Company (AMC), visited us in Rocky Ford. "I hope that you and my sons will be friends, just as your father and I have been." Mr. Miqdadi's words meant a great deal to me as a 27-year-old pup, it was an honor to meet him. Over the past 25 years his sons and I have met in Boston and Los Angeles, in Athens and Seville, in Odessa and Chisinau. Their children have met my children, and my dream is that they will all have even better friendships. On a recent trip an AMC employee said "The AMC-Hollar relationship seems to be more about friendship than business." It might appear that way, but really we are juggling business and friendship.

Our longest relationship is with the Trevino family of Mexico. This family has seen a series of four men named Isidoro. My father sold seed to the first two, the negotiations were always tough. I love them, but these men were tighter than rawhide on the top of a drum. While they were friendly, they had adversarial relationships. Once I started selling to the third Isidoro, things started to be much friendlier. We became such good friends that when he died suddenly, Isidoro IV called me the same day. Two months later I met with the family to discuss their new situation and the future of our business together. We all feel that we are members of each other's families.

Now the Trevinos and I are working together as true partners and our complete faith in each other allows us to make deals without worrying about who will benefit the most. Instead of each of us trying to get a bigger slice of the pie, we work together to make the pie bigger.

In South Africa our family connection is Habe Roode, who has my vote as the world's hardest working seedsman. Habe always remembers some 40-year-old joke between his dad, Chris, and my dad, Vic. Together we have discovered dung beetles, have run out of gas, and introduced market-changing products. We introduce each other to people. We tell each other about our latest new machine or software. We're great friends committed to doing as much business together as possible. All our third generation members will enjoy a very valuable head start, a long history of inter-company trust.

While the chapter title is "Using Family Firm Connections," it does not suggest that you *use* people like this to make a quick buck. On the contrary, you should be committed to a lot of give and take and to having a mutually profitable relationship. Neither can take advantage of the other for very long or the friendship will end. Honesty and integrity are essential here, because negative comments about your actions can last for generations, just as trust and friendship can last for generations.

SUPPORT OTHER FAMILY BUSINESSES

I love going to Van Hook's garden supply store, where I see grandparents working beside their son and grandson. I remember my dad buying trees there when I was 5 years old. My dad and Verne, the grandfather, loved to haggle and discuss the price at great length. Verne's son and I discuss his assortment of shrubs and trees, landscape design, and family business. I buy everything I can from them, rather than the big box store across town, because I like them.

While taking the risk of running out of gas, I'll drive past several chain outlets to get to a Wallace's family owned station. These businesses and others know they have my business because they are a family business. I get better service and convenience from them. They are my connections; someday they can help me with a problem because they've already dealt with it successfully. Even it that doesn't happen, I like gossiping and joking with them. Supporting local business is good business.

OTHER CONNECTIONS

I have also made connections in an unusual way, by hosting young people from other countries. We have hosted young people through youth exchange programs and on behalf of customer-friends. This has given our family knowledge of Spain, Chile, India and Mexico. We have at least one friend in each country now. We had the son of our Spanish customer, and the daughter of our Argentine customer. We look forward to being bound together by much more than business for generations to come.

"Money is like manure;
it's not worth a thing
unless it's spread around
encouraging young things to grow."
– Thornton Wilder

CHAPTER EIGHT

Nurturing Family Financial Advantages

Did you jump ahead to this chapter to learn how to maximize your inheritance? You won't find that advice from this cowboy. The whole idea of getting something for nothing runs contrary to good family business management for future generations. Everyone has to take responsibility to fund their own retirements. Do not count on an inheritance. Contribute to an IRA or other savings vehicles at a young age. Invest in your retirement early and often.

Your real inheritance, should you receive gifts of stock ownership or a job within the company, is the right to work. Your parents want to be a springboard, to help you to get a good start. But after this start, the responsibility is yours. If you do happen to get something through inheritance, accept it as long as you also accept that there is responsibility along with the inheritance. You'll work to continue the business or to increase that inheritance for following generations.

Having said all that, younger family members should not hesitate to ask elders for financial support. As long as you have a reasonable plan and always pay the money back as promised, there is no reason to avoid borrowing — assuming your parents have extra change lying around.

Examples of appropriate requests for loans:
- New business start up
- Erasing high interest debt with a low interest loan
- Education
- Mortgage on home or investment property
- Transfer of stock

Select an interest rate that is a win for both sides. This is not difficult since personal loan and credit card rates are several percentage points higher than one makes in their savings. The IRS has interest rates that they consider to be appropriate for intra-family loans. If no interest were charged, they would argue that a gift was given, and therefore would want some tax on it. They will win the quick argument every time.

Some families have a culture where family loans are forbidden. My family was generous with loans, as long as they were paid back. Other families have their own culture when it comes to money: Are there family trusts to take care of everyone? Did you have a paper route when you were six years old? Whatever your family thinks about money, take that

culture of money out and examine it. Talk about it
with others, even if your family's money culture
includes an unwritten rule to NOT discuss money.
Your circumstances will show you whether an advantage exists. Arrangements should always be done in a
mature way. An arms length agreement should be
written down and followed by both parties. In the
case of a business start up, the agreement should say
what happens in the event of failure.

Our extended family has a history of giving gifts
to grandchildren. Not that we ever had very much to
be giving like this, but savings bonds for education
were popular. Gifts to grandchildren have a double
benefit, they actually are gifts to the middle generation as well.

Great Uncle Merl gave my dad, Vic, a $5,000
loan to buy the first home in Rocky Ford. When
Merl wanted to drill for oil on his ranch, he got the
money and more from Vic. I started buying company stock from Dad by age 26 or so, and he always
carried the loan. The stock was appropriately valued
with discounts for lack of marketability and lack of
control.

If one of the family business connections mentioned in the last chapter comes up with an interesting investment idea, take a risk. Every time someone
offered us a joint venture that was "out of my
league," I refused and regretted it. Examine these
chances closely. Consider mortgaging the farm. Step
up and take your licks in the Big League. How many

chances like this will you get in life? Investigate it, sleep on it, if it feels right in the morning go for it.

WRITE IT DOWN

We've all heard "neither a borrower nor lender be" solemnly spoken as if it were true. After all, it does come from William Shakespeare. However, Shakespeare was an entertainer, not an economist. Great ideas would take much longer to bring to fruition if there were no lending. Giant projects would never be started. How could anyone own their own home without mortgages? When they give the advice "neither a borrower nor lender be" perhaps what they mean to say is "lending money to loved ones is a bad idea because it will lead to hard feelings." Nonsense. If both parties honor the agreement, if it is written down, if conflicts are handled unemotionally, conflict will not occur.

If you want to anticipate conflict resolution, appoint an arbitrator in your original contract. Let's say a father and son agree to start a lawn care business using the father's funds and the son's *sweat equity*. Chances are five or ten years down the road one person may feel slighted. He might try to collect some money to ease the slight. A conflict arises. What to do?

Let someone else fight it out. Let someone else make the decision. Begin any family business venture, loan, or deal with a contract. Include this clause in the contract:

Robert and Bobby McIntyre further agree that their positive relationship as father and son is more important than money. They agree to continue their positive relationship by avoiding conflict. They name J.B. White as arbitrator of any dispute that may arise anyway. They agree to abide by his decision, then to forget about the problem and re-establish their good feelings towards each other. J.B. White will act as an agent of the best interest of the family. As an agent J.B. White will have no personal liability to any involved party.

Under this agreement, any time someone gets bent out of shape he can go and have a chat with Mr. White. He calls the other party and has a chat with him. Perhaps he calls the first one for a cross examination. He reviews the contract or observes the problem. He makes the decision. The parties hug and make up. Your J.B. White doesn't have to be a judge. He could be a trusted family lawyer, outside accountant, Uncle Joe, or businessman. If you have a really big enough deal, you might select a tribunal. A technique like this is less expensive than lawyers and lawsuits. Just the threat of getting a call from J.B. will make both (or all) parties more likely to get along in the first place.

Also, remember your emotional intelligence. If in a family business deal your feelings get hurt, don't spring your feelings onto the other party without warning. If you are at a family dinner, don't just spring the business ball without warning. Whether you are at a family gathering or in your office, begin your conversations with something like this: "As your sister I love you and would do anything for you. I really appreciate the help you've given the family, and it's a pleasure to be in the same family with you. With that in mind, I want to talk about our business deal. We agreed to some things, my expected outcome was different than what I'm getting. When times were hard you asked for more from me and I was happy to give it. Now however, good business practice and my own needs say that I should ask you to pay the loan. Perhaps it is time for you to go to a bank or another family member."

This takes the emotion out of the conversation. The other person's reply may be "I just don't have the money." At that time you have the options of starting legal proceedings, writing off the loan, extending the terms, perhaps rewriting the contract, or helping him to get other funding.

Another thing to remember about arms length agreements, if the terms of the contract change; make a written change in the contract. Do not just agree to it verbally.

In order to handle their estate fairly, some parents give the business to one child, the real estate to another. This is a setup for conflict. Perhaps the son who inherited the real estate feels like he got the smaller half, so he raises the rent. The daughter who is running the business may say "the business can't afford the high rent." This is another case where having an arbitrator named in advance would help. Using emotional intelligence, these two should realize that their parents loved them and wanted to be fair. But fairness is not always possible or even desirable when dividing an estate. We'll return to this topic in the next chapter.

INTRA-PRENEURSHIP

Intra-preneurship is when a company uses the talent of their creative employees to develop innovative products and services — a perfect vehicle for a family firm. While some square pegs may not fit into your round holes, square pegs are still good! If you and your creative son or daughter are not getting along, maybe it's because they are smarter and more up to date than you. If your brother and sister just don't see your business the way you do, allow them the freedom of doing their own thing within the business.

Instead of the "square peg" going off to start her own venture, give her the security of working within the established business. Entrepreneurs within your business are likely to be your best people. They can be hard to keep, and corporate structures are not conducive to creativity. Without creativity, companies have a way of becoming obsolete.

Even if the ideas of your creative person are completely outside your line of work, allow him to use the resources of the company. The resources might be tools or telephones, funding or office space. If the ideas bloom into a separate company, family funding would be less intrusive to ownership than an IPO or venture capital. Take advantage of intra-preneurship, it's a great way for a large company to

Supporting family intra-preneurs diversifies the assets of the family and rejuvenates the company.

exploit small market niches, and to provide meaningful work and responsibility to family members.

Family funding of entrepreneurs or intra-preneurs not only diversifies the assets of the family, but it rejuvenates the company. Imagine a family in the buggy whip business. While the business is going great guns, there is one son who doesn't like working with leather, manufacturing or sales. He might borrow money from the parent or the business to start a corner candy store. As the buggy whip business declines, they can copy the son's success and start a chain of corner candy stores. While that chain is strong, it can fund the grand-daughter's idea to buy the latest hot franchise. When the chain of candy stores starts to decline, they can transfer more assets into the budding chain of franchises.

PERKS

Mmmmmm, perks. Like Homer Simpson slobbering over a donut, family firms are known for taking

some short cuts when it comes to keeping personal and business expenses separate. Such "short cuts" are regarded by the legal system as tax evasion. While Rudolf Giuliani isn't likely to target your business these days like he targeted Leona Helmsley, these perks are not a good idea. In spite of representation by Alan Dershowitz, Helmsley was convicted, and spent 18 months in jail. That is one reason people in my company are not allowed to evade tax. Another reason is fairness. Not all the owners in our business are family members. Not all owners are even employees. If family/manager/owners or anyone is allowed to use company expense for personal gain, they are cheating the other owners.

For that matter, if you have a profit sharing program or year-end bonuses such short cuts would hurt the staff and the future owners. Not to mention, on some days I'm actually proud to pay tax. Without tax, the country doesn't work so well.

Illegal activity aside, what are allowable perks? I've mentioned the feeling of ownership. When your name is on the front of the building, you have a right to feel proud. Beyond just feeling good, the IRS does allow some nice things for us. When the main purpose of your trip is business for three days solid, an extra day for fun is all right. If your spouse serves a verifiable business purpose to attend, the company can pay. But the spouse has to really be taking notes, or speaking, or doing something other than just socializing. Other than the above, my only advice is to consult with your tax accountant. If their advice sounds good, follow it. If it sounds sneaky, get a new accountant.

Perks are especially susceptible to feelings of entitlement. Entitlement was already the focus of my sermon in chapter four, but here is more. If you drive an automobile that belongs to the business, does every family member get the same? If you attend the trade association meeting in Tampa, then lay around on the beach for two days, will your siblings feel just a little resentment? If all family members get company cars and extra long trips, the expense can build up in a hurry. Then when the next generation has 12 family members instead of four, and they are all lapping cream from the company bowl, finances can be strained.

Conspicuous consumption is defined very differently from one family to the next. In some families, Honda is good enough, while others drive nothing but Mercedes. There is nothing wrong with that. Inappropriate purchasing is when you live in a neighborhood of $40,000 homes yet drive an $80,000 vehicle. Inappropriate conspicuous consumption is laying off staff members, and then building a 5,000 square foot home. (I can hear my neighbors saying "Hypocrite! You bought and drove the longest, gaudiest red Cadillac I've ever seen!" Yes, I did some investing in classic automobiles. That is how I know it is such a bad idea!)

RETIREMENT

Long before you go looking in this Family Financial Advantages chapter, you need to take responsibility for your own retirement planning. Talk to an accountant. Read the books. Start early and do not take the money out before retirement. Visit http://money.cnn.com/retirement/ and use their calculator to estimate how much money you need to retire. But, don't get too hung up on the tools — take responsibility. Start a plan, then review it every six months to see how it is working.

If your company is in the start-up phase, the plans for you to consider immediately are:

- Safe Harbor 401(k)
- Individual(k)
- Money Purchase Pension
- Defined Benefit Pension
- Target Benefit Pension
- SEP Plan
- Simple Plans
- Profit Sharing

Having said that, family firms may have some advantages. If you are at retirement age but don't have enough savings, consider a cushy consulting job for the company. Change the buy-sell agreement to make it more in your favor. Arrange to purchase some of the business property, and then lease it back to them. That could guarantee you an income forever, while giving the company some cash during the transition period.

An advisor said to me "Ultimately, it's just a matter of who's tax ox will be gored and when." Start saving early to avoid this juggling, otherwise you will be juggling four balls instead of three.

TAKE ADVANTAGE OF PRIVACY

Unless you are publicly held, your finances are your own business. They aren't published in the Journal. You don't have to hustle to make them look better at the end of each quarter.

Our Procedure Manual has the following, borrowed from another family business (yet, another example of the power of connections).

TOOL BOX:

Sample Privacy Policy

While it is natural to talk about the company you work for, the nature of our business requires some confidentiality. Good judgment should be used in public conversations so that important or secret facts and figures are not mentioned. A good rule of thumb is: If it will possibly help a competitor, hurt a customer or work against your company, do not say it.

We watch interviews with journalists very carefully in this regard. You should ask them for editorial review. You probably won't get it, but it is okay to try. You might be surprised to find what you have blurted out.

Along the same lines, why brag about making a lot of money? This just sets you up for jealousy and ill will. It sets you up for people expecting bigger donations. Anyway, it sure is easier to say, "Business is OK," than to say "We made $450,000 last year, which is 18% ROI and 14% IBITA."

ADVANTAGE: LONG TERM VIEW

Three people aged 20, 40 and 60 have very different concepts about what five years means. Remember what a five-year commitment meant to you when you were 20? But a 60 year old has seen life in several five year chunks, and has participated in 15 year projects. It is hard to conceive of a 50-year time frame until you are a certain age.

The difference in thinking about time isn't just about age. The 60-year-old grandfather, the 40-year-old father and the 20-year-old daughter have different goals. Goals to older people have shorter, or at least, more definite completion dates. A 20- year-old can afford to miss some deadlines, saying, "Ah, I'll get to that next year".

The long term view is a huge advantage of family businesses. Publicly traded corporations have fire sales, work overtime, or announce huge layoffs.

Later they start projects, hire people, and then slash them again when the financial forecast or stock price doesn't look so good. Private companies are more willing to follow through with the original plan, to grind it out. They operate in a smooth fashion, not herky-jerky.

Is a 60-year-old manager likely to approve a 15-year project, knowing that he will retire before the project benefits him? If he has grandchildren in the business he is very likely to approve it.

As an amateur plant breeder, I had several long term projects. Ten years of work trying to alter the flowering pattern of cantaloupes went nowhere. I created hybrids which seemed to go nowhere, then after 15 years caught on in a new market. So I feel that I have a pretty good long-term perspective. If we get an idea to improve a species in January 2000, we'll work on the cross breeding and selection until 2006. This would-be new variety is tested in our gardens in 2007 and 2008. It will be released to cooperators around the world to check adaptability to their climate, which will take two more years. Small orders begin in 2011, larger ones in 2012. Finally in 2013, if we are lucky, very lucky, we might regain our investment. Perhaps one out of 100 plant breeding ideas becomes a best seller. Nine more are also-rans. But, 90 will fail.

At age 52, I know that some of our research programs will not profit me. But when our family business survives into the third generation, I'll take great pleasure in knowing these projects will reward them.

WORKING TOGETHER, THE IDEA-LADEN YOUNGSTER
AND AN EXPERIENCE-LADEN ELDER
MAKE A GREAT TEAM.

While your business may not be research orient-
ed, it should be refreshing itself in other ways — a new
energy efficient refrigerator unit, a large piece of
equipment, or a costly redesign of the product you
manufacture and the retooling of your plant to make
it.

Perhaps a 20-year-old has the great idea for
change but is afraid to make the decision to "gam-
ble" the money. In a family business the 60-year-old
grandfather has had the positive experience of mortgaging everything, then winning. Working together,

105

the idea-laden youngster and an experience-laden elder make a great team.

Such a team may be a rosy picture. What if grandfather constantly vetoes the youngster's ideas? What if all of grandfather's memories are of negative results of chances taken? Grandpa, if you are finding yourself being negative to most of the new ideas that come along, it is time for you to step aside.

Remember the Three Little Pigs when making long-term family business decisions.

The three little piggies had a choice in construction materials. One used straw, one decided on sticks, and the other used brick. The first two were short-term thinkers, while the third must have been thinking about the long-term security of his family. Small towns in our area of south-eastern Colorado were only settled in the 1880s. The countryside is spotted now with useless, dilapidated wooden barns and houses. Even the brick buildings in the middle of town are falling into decay. Even schools, which were built to higher standards, only had a 60 to 80 year life expectancy. Compare that to the great cathedrals of Europe, or to monuments and museums in nations' capitals.

Keep this in mind, when it comes time for your business to build a new building or when you face decisions. Straw would be the cheapest. Wood is moderately expensive and lasts longer. State of the art steel and marble might serve your grandchildren's grandchildren.

There is a threat of an inter-generational dispute here. Grandpa may say, "Hey, wait a minute, I was planning to use that money to take Grandma and me into retirement. Now you want to spend it all on a down payment on the Taj Majal that will take you 50 years to pay off?"

Did you see what just happened with grandpa? He had the business ball in his hand, and then he had the family ball in his hand. His focus changed to his inner family, to himself, in a flash. He said, in effect, "I've forgotten that I was talking as an owner-manager and let my personal needs enter a business conversation." This happens all the time. My great friend, Steve Berg of DeBourg Manufacturing, is fond of saying, "Everything in a family business is a conflict of interest."

This juggling and shifting just needs to be recognized for what it is. It does not have to become a fight. Just recognize it, discuss it, and juggle on.

Don't assume that
if the family is in agreement,
the documents really aren't necessary.

CHAPTER NINE

Taking Advantage
of Legal Issues

U ntil recently I knew as much about the legal background of our corporation as a raccoon knows about the interstate highway system. I had no clue that I could be personally liable for things done in our corporation, or that there are important differences between corporations and other entities. Every shareholder should learn something about these legalities.

Does your business have bylaws and Articles of Incorporation? You should find them or their equivalent, blow the dust off of them, and figure out what they say. Have your lawyer clarify uncertain points. They are the legal backbone of your corporation, and they tell you how many may be on your board, when the shareholders meeting will occur and what it takes to sell your company. They may need to be updated. Good modern lawyers have thought up some good things to add to them to protect individuals.

Protecting yourself as an individual is one big reason why you have a corporation or LLC. Your company is a separate entity, like another person. That entity makes money, pays taxes, and is liable for wrong that it might do. You want yourself to be legally separated from that liability. You want for your home and savings to be safe from the threat of a lawsuit.

I can't tell you the specific things to do in your case of course, your attorney and your documents will tell you that. But in our case I found out about the following.

- Our Articles of Incorporation stipulate that there will be a meeting every year
- The only thing the shareholders do is elect the Board of Directors
- The Board of Directors elects officers
- The officers run the business
- Two thirds of the vote of the Board of Directors can elect to sell our business to an outsider, but that then needs to be approved by a majority of the shareholders
- If the shareholders don't like the action of the Board of Directors, they can call a special meeting and fire them

My dad used to have the opinion that the president of the company should always keep 51% of the business so that the others can't sell the business. He worried about a time when there will be a lot of shareholders that aren't involved in the daily activity of the company. That they might not understand what is going on, and that they could force the sale.

In our case, one person only needs to have 34% ownership in order to block the sale. One person would need to have 67% ownership to be able to single handedly decide to sell the business. What are the figures in your situation? Next week we will vote on whether to change the Article of Incorporation to require 75% agreement of shareholders before the company could be sold.

In a way, my dad was correct. If one shareholder has 51% ownership, he or she can decide who is on the Board of Directors. He or she can fire the Board as well. Again, this is in our case, you need to know the legalities in the case of your business entity.

ADVANTAGE: A GOOD SHAREHOLDERS' MEETING

The first chapter said "As I write, the first member of the third generation is deciding whether to join the firm." Four months later, our son-in-law has decided to join us. This important milestone might not have happened without an informal shareholders meeting. A good shareholders meeting does this:

- Spouses are invited
- Teen-agers are invited
- Someone talks a bit about the history of the company

- Someone talks a bit about how the company is doing, where it is going
- The mission statement is discussed
- The company policy on hiring family is reviewed

Actually this kind of meeting is a hybrid between a shareholders meeting and a family forum. We were looking for any member of the third generation to come to work with us. We needed any and all of them. The last one we expected to step to the plate was our son-in-law, but he did. The next day my daughter said, "All of a sudden, he realized that working in a family business means that your work helps your family, not just some unknown back in the headquarters."

An annual shareholders meeting will be stipulated in your bylaws, and it is different. For that one, you'll have to send out formal invitations. Everyone need not attend, but you have to have a quorum. The shareholders will perform their one and only duty. They will elect the Board of Directors.

BOARD OF DIRECTORS

Even if your business affairs are decided upon by one or two people, you should have actual Board of Directors meetings. The reason for that is to have minutes, so that you have a record of making the big decisions. You made that decision in the hallway or at home? That doesn't matter; put it into the minutes of the board meeting anyway. Why? Minutes become a history of your company. In 50 or 75 years, things will be forgotten. Later someone will be interested in the history. Reviewing the minutes will show them why you made the decisions that you made. They will show when someone was named president, who made the decision to sell part of the company outside, or what the thinking was when other important crossroads were approached.

Minutes are even more important for another reason. They show that you acted as a corporation, not as an individual. When the IRS comes to audit you, or a lawyer arrives to sue you, the first thing they do is demand to see the minutes of your corporate board meetings. If you can't show that you acted as a corporation, they will sue you as individuals. One purpose of having a corporation is to shield you from personal liability. Act like a corporation by having board meetings and minutes in order to protect your personal assets.

ESTATE PLANNING

If you are as old as me, you may remember a classic Volkswagen TV ad. A line of limousines and other expensive cars slowly followed a hearse in a funeral procession. A strong voice reads the will. As each person's name is read a well-dressed person appears in his or her car. The will lists things like: "To my brother Wynnewood, who never knew the value of a dollar, I leave one dollar." One greedy family member got "one red cent." Finally, there is an old

Volkswagen beetle being driven by a young man. To this young man, the voice reads, "To my nephew Fred who has lived his life frugally, I leave my entire fortune of $14 million."

The deceased obviously believed that one should be frugal, should not seek to get something for nothing. He had the right to do the unexpected in his will. Apparently he disliked his family so much that he didn't care about their feelings, about the disturbance that such a will is sure to cause.

If you are a family-business owner and do care about the goodwill in your family, it is never too soon to think about how the ownership will move into the next generation. We've all heard stories about a company founder who built a big business. Some of his children join the business and stay with it for years, while some of his children do not join the business. When it comes time to write a will, the founder is faced with a dilemma: "I don't have much to leave in this will except the business. The business is worth more than my house, savings, and miscellaneous. How can I give equally to my children?"

There are many ways this dilemma can be answered. The founder could sell the business, and then divide the liquid assets equally among the children. This, however, means that the business leaves the family. While its sales price will support the family, once that is gone, it is gone. This answer is not fair to the child who has worked and contributed to the business.

So, a second solution is to give unequal gifts. That doesn't sit well with some heirs, or parents. Perhaps the wise person will state in their will that: "Sally is to get a higher percent of the funds generated by the sale of the company because she worked there for 15 years, not because I love her more than Paul. I love my children equally." If Paul chooses not to believe his parent's words, that is his personal problem.

Another solution: Give company stock to non-employee family members. This answer sets up the siblings in a partnership. One or more are owner/managers. One or more are outside owners. Over time, those inside the business can buy out the others, if it is profitable enough. Some are uncomfortable with this answer, visualizing nothing but disagreements. But I've known siblings who became teams that made it work. Personally I don't think its right for the parent to try to control things from the grave. Give the children the fun of juggling!

"Fair, but not equal" is an approach suggested by Dr. Ron Hanson, a respected University of Nebraska professor, who has studied family business from the farm and ranch perspective for 30 years. He teaches that "you can replace the farm, but you can't replace the family." He counsels that one doesn't have to give equally to all the children to be fair, suggesting that perhaps *fair* is not equal. Equitable giving is better. For example, a ranchman has two sons. One stays on the ranch, putting in 20 years of sweat equity. The other leaves for another occupation. It may be equitable to leave the ranch to one son, and leave an insurance policy or something else to the second. The second does have blood equity, after all.

"Fair, but not equal . . ."
suggests family-business expert Dr. Ron Hanson.
You don't have to give equally
to all the children to be fair.

I also have my personal solution to this dilemma, one derived from years of study and thought. Well, it's not really a solution but more of a philosophy. I firmly believe that everyone is completely free to make his will exactly in the way that he chooses, without asking anyone his opinion. The gifts, if any, do not have to be equal. Children of anyone deserve to be nurtured until adulthood, loved forever, supported during as much educational time as practical to their abilities (and possible for the parents to afford), and allowed the right to work and to love. No one should feel entitled to an inheritance. I believe that a big inheritance might not be a good thing for a person. Doesn't that deprive him of the right to work?

So, my philosophy is that it is all right for a person to make unequal gifts to their children — or no gifts at all. The decision is up to the individual. On the other hand, gifts to people in your will that are equal would be nice. If you strongly believe that the gifts should be equal, you'll need to downsize your business. Get better balance in your estate among the business, outside investments, life insurance, and home. Getting such balance might take several years, so it is not too early to start planning. Besides, planning your estate early is a great idea to avoid paying undue taxes.

I believe that a family business, or in our case a closely held business, exists for the benefit of its owners first, then for the benefit of the owners' families. Family members who are neither employees nor owners also have rights. As stakeholders, as people whose name is associated with the business, and as family members whose lives have been affected by the business, they deserve information about the business. They deserve the right to talk about the interaction between the family and the business. But this is an idea that will be discussed in the "Tools" chapter under "Family Forum."

CONTRACTS

Employment contracts are one example of a kind of contract that is helpful in family business. They should give some security to both parties. They can help when hiring in-laws or immediate family. Drafting, writing and discussing them will bring up good questions. Like all contracts, a big purpose is to correct faulty memories.

You'll want some kinds of contracts; they help avoid misunderstandings. When well written, they say who is to do what. Write the simple ones yourself; go to a good attorney for complex issues. Keep them informal and short. Call it a memorandum of agreement instead of a contract. Don't get bogged down in a lot of "what ifs." Use old agreements as guides.

But, do remember that contracts aren't the end-all of the business world. Say you have an agreement to cooperate with a competitor on a project. You bring in your great lawyer who puts it all down in a 30-page contract. The contract is designed to protect you. Nonetheless, your competitor can always bring in a better lawyer and find a way to break the contract. My friend Erroll Pullen, the inventor of Prev-Am, says: "Paper is only as good as the man that stands behind it."

BUY-SELL AGREEMENT

Also known as a Stock Restriction Agreement, this is a legal document that spells out what happens to ownership in the event of the death of a shareholder. It might say that you have to offer to sell your shares to your partner instead of selling them to an outsider. It might stipulate who may own stock, and prevent you from using your shares as collateral.

You'll want a good lawyer in on this one. This kind of legal document is mainly used by two partners starting a business. If you are in your second or third generation, you should take a hard look at yours. Compare what it says and what it might do to ownership as compared to your group's vision for the company. (We'll come back to vision.)

My fellow shareholders and I are wrestling with this issue today as it happens. We had one agreement, and were just presented with a draft of a new one by our attorney. One of my brothers and I just had a conversation that went like this: "I was able to read this one at least. It says we can't just give our stock away to our kids without offering it back to the corporation first."

"Well, that's because you wanted it both ways. You wanted to be able to give it to your kids, but also for the Board to be able to block the sale of stock to certain people. If the Board can block the sale to an outsider, they have the right to block your gift, or mine."

"The attorney is suggesting a new valuation system. We'll have to look at that from different perspectives."

"Yes, it will decide whose tax ox gets gored and when."

"I still think the fact that we can't borrow against our shares makes them less valuable. Seems to me, if you own something you ought to be able to leverage its value by using it as collateral."

"You are right, but if you want to protect the company from being taken away from the current shareholders, it makes sense. All it would take would be for one of the major shareholders to have a personal bankruptcy, and then all of a sudden we'd have a banker trying to tell us how to run our business."

"Well, I don't think they would get very far, let them have at it! But, let's seriously consider whether we need one of these things at all. I trust the next generation of shareholders to be trustworthy, to handle ownership of the stock in a responsible way."

"I agree. And I don't believe in trying to run the company for future generations. Let's say that 50 years from now there are 16 cousins that own the stock. Seven of them gang up on the other nine and sell 40% of the company to a competitor. In my opinion it is up to the nine cousins to have better educated the seven as to why the company should remain closely held. I don't think it is fair for us to keep them from having the fun of the argument."

"Right, and by that time we'll be moldering in our graves."

"Right, all we can do is the best we can while we are above ground. Let's sleep on this idea, then strongly consider just tearing it up."

The idea that we should not try to control the future generations through any legal document came directly from our company attorney. Before my conversation with him, I had our founder's philosophy. He liked to say, "One person, probably the president or other experienced manager, needs to keep 51% of the company so that he or she can make all the decisions. That person has been me, and it is going to be you."

Under that scenario the future of the business, including the decision to sell it, rests with one person. Yes, this person knows the most about the business, and they have the vision. Yes, this person could evolve into a team, like we have, made up of several people with complete trust in each other. But whether 51% is held by one person, two, five or 75 people, they still might decide to sell the business. Aren't the odds better that one person could make a wrong decision than a group of 75?

> *Don't use legal documents to control your company for future generations.*

Let's say that I am the current beneficent dictator, owning 51% and calling all the shots. Maybe my life goes haywire all of a sudden. Say I get recalled from the school board in an ugly controversy. (Happened) Say I go through a divorce. (Won't happen) That I get just a little bit mentally ill. (Who knows?) In spite of my rapidly changing mental, emotional and financial stresses I'm still calling the shots. Boom, our business is sold overnight.

In my opinion, it's better to have lots of owners, rationally discussing the best interests of the business and the family. This vision thing is way overworked. We don't have vision. I can *visualize* what I'll have for dinner then take steps to make that happen, but I can't predict our sales and profits two years in advance, let alone 20 years in advance. So why try to tie the hands of future generations? All that you can do is the best that you can do while you are above ground. Realize that future generations deserve to juggle on. Educate them while you can, then step aside.

In the end we did adopt a new Shareholders Agreement. The *raisin d'etre* was that two shareholders think of their shares as a kind of life insurance with their spouses as beneficiaries. They didn't want the spouse to have to negotiate with the other owners over value and payment. The other owners weren't opposed to the idea of having these particular spouses as shareholders; they were just mildly opposed to the idea of non-management shareholders in theory.

The second reason we have a Shareholders Agreement is to avoid the Crocodile Effect, which will be explained in Chapter 12.

PERSONAL LIABILITY

Finally, when you sign, for example, the lease committing your company to pay the leaser every month, did you sign it as an individual? Sign "On behalf of Your Company, Inc. by (*your signature*)," or you have committed yourself as an individual to honor the terms of the lease. Again, one of the main reasons to have a corporation, LLC or LLP is to limit your personal liability.

Similarly, if you are checking someone into the hospital, you may be asked to fill in a form. If they ask for a signature, write in the other person's name, then "by (*your signature*)." Just signing it makes you liable to pay the hospital bill.

"If you are failing to plan,
you are planning to fail."
— Tariq Siddique

CHAPTER TEN

Using Tools
to Your Advantage

Take a moment to think about your family business. Ask yourself if you are professional in how you go about making decisions. Are you professional in the way that family members treat each other? Compare your business's inner workings to other businesses around you. Does it seem as professional as theirs? Is your machinery well lubricated?

As your business evolves from *start-up* to *expansion* to *maturity*, it may benefit from some tools that have never been used before. It is fine that the founder is making all the decisions during the start-up phase, but as the business grows that should change. If you are having a difficult time with a decision or a situation, you should consider this list of tools. Select one, give it a try.

- Family Forum
- Code of Conduct
- Family Hiring Policy
- Paid Advisors

- Consultants
- Board of Advisors
- Successor's Binder

ADVANTAGE: THE FAMILY FORUM

All the other books on this subject agree on only one thing: "If you have more money than you know what to do with, hire me, the author/consultant." No, wait, I'm just kidding. They agree on this one: Having a Family Forum (or Family Council) is the single best tool for survival. It promotes accord between the business leaders and the family. It leads to a balanced development of the family and the business.

Sounds like a great idea. We have never had one. But it is on our agenda for next year. We have not been breaking this rule on purpose. It is just that up until now our group has not been complex enough to require it. Or, we just didn't like the idea of having family around. Does that sound like you?

It would be much better to start one during a period of calm and agreement within the family, as opposed to using this tool as a cure for a disagreement. Get used to meeting as a family, having some fun along with some instructional time.

Your Family Forum might discuss a major business idea, and then send the results of the discussion to the board of directors. Whether the board acts on the family advice is up to the board.

The Family Forum has become such a serious tool that Loyola University offered a course in how to be your own facilitator at such a meeting, and the course had 60 hours of training! They teach such things as how to handle conflict and how task-oriented businessmen should back off and allow emotion-oriented family members enough room to speak. Your business might leave the facilitation to a professional. It might choose a family member who is not in the business to be the facilitator. If the business leader also tries to lead the family through this Forum, that leader will be juggling all weekend.

CODE OF CONDUCT

Sounds rather starchy, doesn't it? But a Code of Conduct is a good tool, and it professionalizes your business and helps family members to mature. It also lays all the expectations on the table. It can be written by your business leader, or better, it is something that a group could work on during a family retreat or forum. Details of proper conduct will vary among businesses. For example, the details wouldn't be the same for a dairy as for a pair of lawyers. But in general what everyone will be aiming at is to act like a business person while on the job, leaving the family baggage at the door. Or the Code may ask you to announce it, when all of a sudden, you start talking about the family ball while you are at work.

> ## TOOL BOX:
>
> *Sample Code of Conduct*
>
> - We will support each other in front of other employees.
>
> - We will not judge each other.
>
> - We will not take any assets out of the business except as salary and formal benefits, these benefits to be determined by the board of directors.
>
> - We will publicly recognize the accomplishments of each family employee.
>
> - We will maintain family and work boundaries, avoiding discussion of business at family functions.

FAMILY HIRING POLICY

We call ours the Nepotism Policy. You might choose to adopt one. It is something that should be explained to young family members, and is something that can be discussed at the Family Forum. Our policy was borrowed from a magazine article, and then changed over the years. Yours might be more family friendly, or it might be even more "strictly business."

TOOL BOX:

Sample Nepotism Policy

- Family members must meet the same criteria for hiring as non-family applicants.

- Family members are expected to meet the same performance level required of non-family members.

- As a general principle, family members will be supervised by non-family members.

- Family members may not be hired by their closest relative. Family members may be offered a 12-month internship by the board of directors. Then a committee of three will make a recommendation to the Board whether or not to offer full-time employment. A second 12 month internship might be advisable. Compensation will be at fair market value for the position held.

- Family members are encouraged to get work experience outside the company before applying. Their work experience will be a guiding factor in the decision whether to hire.

PAID ADVISORS

Advice from a good attorney at any price can be money well spent. When you absolutely have to learn about a legal situation, spend the money.

You already know me, that I prefer using family firm connections to spending money. But they don't call attorneys and CPAs professionals for nothing. They spend a lot of time keeping themselves up to date on important knowledge. You are paying for their time with you, and also for their study time. It can be a bargain.

When hiring any advisor everyone should be clear on who is the client. Often the advisor works for the company, but he could represent the Board, the third generation members as a group, or an individual. If the business is paying the bill, it wouldn't be right for you to ask him to help you to pull one over on cousin Pete. If you need help to do that, hire your own advisor.

CONSULTANTS

Don't you just love listening to consultants? They always have great new catch phrases. They drop names of famous clients. They have clever ideas and are good listeners. If your business is very large, you'll need consultants. If you have complex questions about chemical waste or metallurgy, you may need temporary outside help. You may want a family business expert to speak at your Family Forum.

But hiring consultants to help make decisions? Or to improve the relationships among family members? Top consultants in the field charge a couple thousand dollars a day, and they'll need some days just to ask background questions. If your business is big enough and has enough problems, go for this tool. Just remember, you should be the one to make the decision, not them. Why not just make the decision? Are you hiring them to make the family happier? Really? Just make the family happier. If you need to improve relationships, work to improve relationships by talking to each other, not by putting a consultant into the mix. Should I ever become a consultant, heaven forbid, remind me to print an amended second edition for this paragraph!

BOARD OF OUTSIDE ADVISORS

Let's imagine that you are a 55- year-old controlling owner. You have a son and a daughter working in your business. You see the cloud on the horizon. "I have to select one over the other to succeed me. I don't want to make that decision; someone will be hurt by it. I'm going to select, hire and train a Board of Advisors and let them make the decision."

So you go down your list of peers and friends. You contact some of them and form this board. You spend a lot of time preparing presentations, so that this board knows everything about your business and your children. Once they know as much as you can teach them, you ask them to select one successor. This board will hem and haw, ask a lot more questions, interview the children and delay. The children might very well be put off by the process.

After all the time and money invested, this board is going to do one of three things. They'll say that they can't make the decision, and that you have to. Or they will pick the one that you do not prefer. Perhaps you'll get lucky and they select the one that you knew in your heart is better. Why didn't you just make that decision yourself?

You knew the answer. You should have pulled the trigger.

Waiting for too much advice
is often an excuse for not making a decision.

And by the way, how about starting the process by asking the son and daughter who should be the next boss? Probably they had the solution figured out already.

Having said that, boards of outside advisors can be a very powerful tool. At least that is what I've read, and I believe it. But they will expect pay and liability insurance. If you have a profitable business and lots of problems, go for it. For those without the resources, here is another idea. Create an imaginary board. Imagine that you have hotshots from Microsoft and General Motors, along with some of your wise friends and relatives. Prepare the presentation that you'll give them. Prepare the graphs and describe your business problem.

Trust me, by the time you have prepared the presentation, the best answer will appear to you. When you have the wise answer, pull the trigger. Waiting for too much advice might just be an excuse for not making the decision. I learned this trick while preparing to present problems to an advisory group. At least half the time, the answer came to me before the meeting. The rest of the time they told me to select the path that I'd been avoiding because it involved the hard stuff. I had been resisting that answer because it was hard for me. The different perspective of outside advisors can be a powerful help, they not only push you along the tightrope but give you a safety net as well.

SUCCESSION PLAN

Your emotional leader might be called upon to help form a succession plan, or at least, to get an elder leader thinking about how succession is inevitable. Naturally the business leaders should act as a team to develop the details of training, transfer of ownership, and timing of change.

Succession of leadership is more than just the transfer of the president's title. It is a process, not an event. In my case, the process has lasted for 30 years. The process of turning my responsibilities over to the next generation has begun before all responsibility has been turned over to me. In other words, having my father in the next office every day means that his opinion still counts. Believe me I am not complaining, it is better to lose the wise advice of a father/leader later rather than sooner.

Our case is not unique in the seed industry. We know two seed companies where the father was unlocking the front door every morning at age 95. The sons were considering retirement before the fathers.

We tease my dad, Vic, about this. At his 75th birthday party we told him that we'd changed the locks, that he wouldn't be getting a new key. His present was a scrapbook. Last week we told him: Our company slogan this year is "88 and out the gate." We are only teasing him. Vic has been great at turning over responsibility. Whether he is physically present in our offices for the next 20 years doesn't make a lot of difference at this point, because we'll always remember his advice. His truisms and beliefs will never be forgotten.

As mentioned, hanging around too long can be a negative thing of course. Young people want responsibility. The prospect of having to serve a 30 year internship is just too onerous for a 28 year old to contemplate. It isn't fair.

During one of the screening interviews with our son-in-law, my brother Andy sprung the question on me "When are you going to retire?" The thought "When I'm damn good and ready" sprang to mind and was discarded. I stammered out something like "Once the next generation is trained and once my retirement is funded." Which is a good answer, but it is also a cop-out. Our son Cody has teased me about missing my first two retirement dates, age 40 (what a dreamer!) and age 50 (dream on). I realized that by not setting a date, by not setting a goal down in writing, I was setting myself up for future delays. So I said "Okay, let's say 10 years from today."

Such a commitment will force us to hire and train successors. It will force owners to start selling stock to fund retirement. My electronic calendar now has annual reminders such as "three years to go, are you getting ready?"

Whatever the situation in your business, start working on a succession plan. It is vital if the business is expected to continue. You can't just stand on the tightrope, you have to keep walking.

SUCCESSOR'S BINDER

This tool is for anyone. It has been extremely valuable to me.

I keep a binder that will serve as a guide book for my successor, or for my replacement. Whenever I have a thought that I consider to be worth keeping, I write a memo into this binder. If a staff member writes an especially effective sales letter, it goes into the binder. Columns or parts of newsletters are photocopied and inserted. Our binder is broken down into these sections: Mission and Vision Statements,

Financial Planning, Marketing, Sales, Production, Research, Personnel, Ownership and Miscellaneous.

Such a tool becomes a source of ideas. When you fall off the tightrope, this binder can be used as a springboard to get back on.

Similarly, my electronic calendar is filled with reminders and nuggets of wisdom. While our business might be especially seasonal, annual reminders are great business tools. For years we were unhappy with the printing date of our price list. Simply putting a repeating annual note in the calendar on January first solved the problem. It says "starting the price list is something you love to procrastinate. Here is the process; do it this week."

As you work, consider what would happen to your business should you suddenly not be there. Does that thought make you want to organize your files better? Everyone likes to keep secrets because that adds power. It adds mystique to your position. But someday you'll have to train your successor.

Mine is labeled "Cody's Binder." Cody Hollar and Audrey Hervouet were married in her home town in France. The weekend was a wonderful event because it united those two, the two families, and all the French and Americans that were there. Cody is following the expert's advice to get outside experience before considering a job within the family business. Cody and I both contribute to the binder, we've studied it together, not since birth but for several years.

Just because the binder is labeled with his name, that doesn't mean that the leadership is reserved for him. He and his brother-in-law and others will have some juggling of their own to do.

DON'T GET BOGGED DOWN BY USING TOO MANY TOOLS.

HOW MANY TOOLS ARE YOU USING . . . HOW MANY TOOLS ARE USING YOU?

Just remember that a great advantage of closely held firms is that they are not bogged down with things that are institutionalized in the big public companies. I hope that this list of tools is helpful to you, but having too many is a burden.

Too many tools can slow your business down. Examine your business to make sure it is lean and agile. Even if a tool is extremely helpful to you, resist the temptation to *institutionalize* it.

Imagine your company president gone two days per month for TEC, your CFO gone 15% of the time at seminars, four board of directors meetings per year, 3 shareholders meetings per year, 2 family retreats per year, and two active consultants. What time does this leave to do the business of your business?

Use the tool then put it back on the pegboard while you concentrate on operating your business or doing your job within it. Stay lean and agile.

Your choice of tools will have much to do with how old and complex your business is. The size of your business, the number of employees, the number of owners will help you decide which level of organization is best. Be aware that if you have a lot of institutionalized tools, you may use them as a crutch. Every time a decision presents itself, you'll say: "Let's leave that for the BOD meeting." Or, "Let's bring in another consultant." Or, "Let's begin another series of meetings." You'll start hiring consultants to figure our how much you're spending on consultants. Ask yourself if your business would be better if it were quicker. Are you deferring the decisions too much? Start walking that tightrope a little faster, juggle on.

Don't sell the goose;
sell the eggs.

CHAPTER ELEVEN

Keeping Ownership Close

The ownership ball needs to be both tossed and caught — always in accord with the family and the business. Let's examine the benefits and responsibilities of ownership. What does ownership mean to you?

Ownership is the least understood of the three things being juggled. My dictionary can't seem to define it without putting the word into the definition: "ownership is the state of being an owner" and "the legal right of possession." Possession *is* ownership. To me, ownership can bestow benefits, while also bringing responsibilities. Let's examine both the possible benefits and responsibilities associated with ownership.

BENEFITS OF OWNERSHIP

Ask four shareholders "What do you expect from ownership?" and you might hear very diverse answers:

SHAREHOLDER 1: I expect the same from the family business as from investments in the stock market, namely an increase in value of the stock and dividends. It is an insur-

141

ance policy for my spouse, or if I live long enough, to fund our retirement. So I need performance from this stock.

SHAREHOLDER 2: With my 51% ownership, I expect control. I'll determine who is on the Board of Directors, I'll decide whether the business will be sold, I'll even determine who the next controlling owner will be.

SHAREHOLDER 3: As a son-in-law, ownership is proof of acceptance into the family.

SHAREHOLDER 4: As a non-family manager, my shares are a golden parachute.

Reducing each answer down to one word, we find what they are looking for from ownership. Money. Control. Acceptance. Protection. Four simple words, each of which carries a ton of emotional weight. Each of which is considered a benefit of ownership.

Even a very small percentage of the ownership can and should mean a great deal to an owner. While it might not mean the world, it can be very emotional. That is why it is so important for the owners to sit down together occasionally and discuss ownership. Everyone should be asked what their goals are for the company. What are their plans for their shares?

Ask yourself: Which of the four benefits of ownership apply to me? Are you having trouble deciding what ownership means to you? Join the crowd, we are all schizophrenic on this idea. Here are some tips for deciding what ownership ultimately means to you. Find out if you are bound by a Buy-Sell Agreement and understand that document. Ask the major shareholders what their dreams are for their shares. Discuss ownership with the older generation. These conversations will probably lead into the topics of survival into the next generation and the succession plan.

Earlier I mentioned the Crocodile Effect. It was explained to me by Francois Delescluse, in Lyon, France. A crocodile lurks by the bank of the river, then lunges out and grabs the foot of a passing gazelle. Its powerful clinched jaws hold the victim, the crocodile has great patience. The gazelle eventually gets tired and stops thrashing. The crocodile then gets a new grip higher and higher. You get the idea.

*Selling a minority interest in a family business
to a big outsider
can create the Crocodile Effect.*

Mssr. Delescluse used this story as a warning to never sell a minority interest in the family business to a big outsider. While the big outsider may have some wonderful "strategic plans for a mutually beneficial partnership," what they really have in mind is a take-over. Their hidden agenda is control. To them a minority interest in a smaller company only means that they have the hoof of the gazelle. Francois knew this to be true from experience. This is one big reason that we have a Buy-Sell Agreement.

THE LEGACY SPEECH

Some owners are whole hog into the idea of continuing the family business in perpetuity. They'll say: "I'll use my position as shareholder, family member and manager to train the next generations to be caretakers of the business . . . to cherish ownership and the business in such a way that they can pass it on to their heirs in better financial shape, with a better reputation, than when they got it. This business will last forever, nourish our family and our family will always own it."

At Hollar Seeds we call this the Legacy Speech. But let's get real here, folks. While the inheritance tax laws in the U.S. are currently improving, it takes a lot of profit to fund successions. Not every business, not every industry, not every family is going to make that kind of money. Not every family will always have the desire to work together.

I have been laying the Legacy Speech on everyone at our shareholder's meetings. I have told my children, "When you own more shares and become an experienced manager, you can decide for yourself whether you'll give the next generations the Legacy Speech, or whether you'll sell the company, or whether you'll do something else." My brother

Andy has different feelings about the Legacy Speech, he suggested, "My advice is to throw the Legacy Speech in the trash."

Whoa, there Brother Hollar. The Legacy Speech was created by the professors who wrote the textbooks on family business management, and by families in the Old World that have existed in business for many generations. It is practically the law that authors on the subject, whether in columns, magazines or books, finish up with — the mushy part about creating an eternal legacy.

Let's examine the Legacy Speech with different wording:

> *You will only be a caretaker, not a real owner. You will leave the business in better shape than when you got it or you'll bring disgrace upon yourself. No one deserves to own the business for their own benefit. You'll work here all your life. You must put the health of the business before your own well-being, and that of your closest loved ones.*

Ownership with that many stipulations makes it a lead parachute. It isn't fair for one generation, who might have had a favorable financial environment, to put that much responsibility on the next generation who will certainly have it tougher. Even if your business has been highly profitable for generations while maintaining market share, in today's world whole industries have become obsolete, *toute suite* . . . let alone businesses.

Ultimately, ownership should give you freedom. Owning one share of any business gives you the right to attend the shareholder's meeting and to be listened to at that meeting. Unless you are bound by a Buy-Sell Agreement, you have the right to give or

Ownership with too many stipulations
is a lead parachute.

sell that share to whoever you please. Most importantly, it gives you the right to be your own boss, in effect. "I work in MY company. My work benefits me as an owner." The decision is yours, but in my case, I'm listening to my brother and cooling it with the Legacy Speech. As mentioned before, why try to run the business for future generations? All you can do is the best you can do while it is your turn on the tightrope.

RESPONSIBILITIES OF OWNERSHIP

What does an owner actually do? Arrive at work late because they are not beholden to anyone? Or be at work early and late, because they care more about the business? Does an owner milk the company's profit, or selflessly support the business, staff and community?

As an owner, you are free to attempt any of the above benefits of ownership. All that owners really have to do, their only responsibility, is to appoint the leadership of the business. That was mentioned in Chapter Nine among other legal issues. The owners (shareholders) elect the board of directors, which elects officers. The officers either run the business or appoint someone to do that. Completing the circle, if the owners are not happy with how the business is being run, they elect a new board of directors so that the leadership changes.

First and second generation companies usually do not think in those terms, they usually have a clear leader and majority owner. Even if your business only has two people as owner/managers, the bottom line responsibility of ownership is selecting who will run your business. "That's easy, I'm going to run it," says the founder, which is probably a good idea until the founder becomes less competent at that than someone else would be.

"That's easy, I get to run it next because I'm the only child of the founder," says the next generation, which is a false assumption. The owner will appoint whoever they choose.

In the second, third and later generations the ownership is likely to be split up among several owners. When that is the case, the chance for a proxy fight occurs. When that is the case, it is the responsibility of any owner to be knowledgeable about the business, the industry, and the leadership. Furthermore, it is the responsibility of majority shareholders to keep minority shareholders informed about the same things.

"To put the world right in order,
we must first put the nation in order;
to put the nation in order,
we must first put the family in order;
to put the family in order,
we must first cultivate our personal life;
we must first set our hearts right."
— Confucius

CHAPTER TWELVE

Keeping the Family Closer

I write a column about family business for a magazine that represents the Southeastern region of Colorado where I live. For the past two years, I have posed this following riddle in my column: *What comes first, the business or the family?*

Our own personal answer to this question underlies many decisions we make. Answering it correctly lies at the heart of successful family business management. While the answer is neither "family" nor "business" every time, some managers obviously lean more in one direction than another.

Taking the idea *in extremis* gives us two imaginary companies. The business first company grows rapidly. Family staff members are underpaid, unhappy and tend to find other jobs. The owner finds himself at retirement time with a large business and a small family. Which family member has the savings to buy it? Or who can afford to pay the inheritance tax?

The second company is completely family first. Salaries are too large, the company never takes risks nor grows.

Family members are spoiled by always getting what they want. Perhaps they are less happy than those in the first example because the business keeps going downhill.

While it becomes evident that the answer is "Let's take a middle road, let's consider each decision on its own. Let's strive for a contented family that supports and is supported by a financially healthy business," how exactly can we do that?

Just as "What comes first, the chicken or the egg?" is a trick question, so is this: "What comes first, the business or the family?" The answer to the chicken question is *mu*, which means *your question cannot be answered because it depends on incorrect assumptions.* The answer to the family business question is: Family commitment comes first.

However, the steps down the middle road to happiness are: Commitment, Needs Assessment, Action, Repeat the first three.

COMMITMENT

Good managers are cheerleaders, coaches and quarterbacks. They are team captains that inspire their key players to sacrifice and to perform. They work in any manner of ways, employing all the tools available to them. Staff meetings, personal chats during coffee, compliments, rewards and newsletters. They share their vision for the future of the company, and somehow get everyone to agree to that vision.

Or they don't. Maybe *none* of the family is on the Clue Train. They don't even know where to buy tickets, and your informational seminars and weekend retreats aren't getting it done. If key family employees are simply not sharing the same vision, then perhaps it is time to make a family first decision or two. Or perhaps they call the manager to task, saying "Back off, Grump, you are obsessed with the business and we as a family need your presence and love more often." Again, time to decide in favor of family.

NEEDS ASSESSMENT

What do family members need now? More responsibility or more pay? More vacation or a trip behind the barn for a whipping? The owner-manager or the managing team might have a guess, but in some cases they are going to have to sit down and ask the family member. I know that is yucky, having the old heart to heart talk which just might start an argument. But the only way to get to cooperation is through understanding.

What does the business need now? A different strategy or product? An infusion of cash at the expense of year end bonus? A new staff member with qualifications that no current family staff member has?

ACTION

Now the manager has the necessary information.
The decision will be made based upon the commitment level of his family members, their needs and
the needs of the business. One time the decision
will lean towards supporting the family, the next
time it will support the business. When supporting
the business, one can say: "If you'll skip this year's
bonus and help me to expand sales by 10%, then
next year you'll be rewarded."

REPEAT

More quickly than we'd like, another decision comes
up. Perhaps even a gut-wrenching dilemma. Just take
a deep breath and start the process over again.

Your business can thrive while having resources
on hand in case of family emergency. You can man-
age your company down the middle road by gaining
commitment, assessing the needs of family and business, then making rational decisions accordingly.

While working on this book, I realized that this column neatly side-steps the question. Perhaps "taking
the middle road" is good family business management, but something about it is unsatisfying. So, I
tackled the riddle again and realized what most of
you probably already knew: Of course, the family
comes first!

What do you do when the decision is really critical, when there is no chance to take the middle

road? Who do you choose, your business or your family. My firm opinion now is that critical decisions involving both family and business interests should be made to protect and nurture your family.

The title of this book *Keep Your Business Close and Your Family Closer* comes from Mario Puzo's Godfather II. The brilliant strategist and the quintessential business family said: "Keep your friends close, but keep your enemies even closer." They meant that enemies cannot be trusted, so you have to keep a close eye on them. I do not mean to equate family with enemies, just the opposite in fact. I've mentioned our son-in-law a couple of times. By now, he has decided to come to work for us.

*Always remember that
your family existed before the business.
And, your family will exist
after the business is gone.*

Everyone is delighted to have Andy Medina in the business. He is in town now, arranging to buy a home. Our daughter Andrea and my wife are buying a Curves franchise, which fits in nicely with my thoughts in Chapter Eight. They are in Texas this week to attend the Curves management training course. Andy has already helped me by coming up with the title for this book. Andrea picked the name for our web site: www.fambizjuggler.com. And my wife Helen has been a very important source of wisdom for this book . . . and for life.

I realized that maybe I needed to ask a different question. Another movie reminded me of the question: "What is thicker, blood or water?" The answer came to me as I remembered giving away my daughter at her wedding, my own wedding, and my mother Laura. Blood *is* thicker than water. This is not just sentimentality; it is logical. Why did you start or enter the business? It was for the benefit of your family. The real questions should be:

Do you work for the welfare of the business,
or
Do you work for the welfare of the family?

You work for the continuation of the family, the pleasure, the love, the benefit of the family. That is the bottom line. You sacrifice the business, you sacrifice the money, you sacrifice your life if need be, you sacrifice everything for the benefit of your family.

I've worked with many of my company's staff members for decades. They have become virtual family members, and their welfare often comes before the welfare of the business. Several customers and I are close enough to feel that we are in each other's families. I'll often favor a customer over the business, so why not do the same for family?

After all, why was your business started? It was for the benefit of your family. Money is money, but it is not the goal; it is only a tool. It is the tool that your business uses to make your family comfortable. Your family existed before your business. It will exist when your business is gone.

The essence of life is love. The best and easiest way to have love is to give it away to your family. Walk the tightrope, work towards making money. But always remember, you are working for the family, you are working for fun, you are working for love.

Here is my business rendition of The Serenity Prayer:

> *Handle your work in a business-like way,*
> *Be with family in a loving atmosphere,*
> *Treat ownership with respect.*
> *God, please grant me the wisdom to always know the*
> *difference.*

Juggling three complex things while walking the tightrope of life is an extremely satisfying pursuit. Great-uncle Merl Axford was a pretty good juggler, and you can be too. Just practice a while, you'll get better. Good luck to you as you seek balance in your life.

A tongue in cheek guide
to terms used in this book.

APPENDIX

Glossary

BLOOD EQUITY: rights or opportunities because you are a family member

CODE OF CONDUCT: a set of rules for family members that are working together. See sample on page 126.

CROCODILE EFFECT: tendency for large companies to buy a minority interest in a family business, then to eventually gobble them up.

EMOTIONAL INTELLIGENCE: ability to understand people and to understand yourself, as opposed to your Intelligence Quotient or I.Q., which only measures your book smarts.

EMOTIONAL LEADER: someone who is trusted for discussions of personal matters.

ENTITLEMENT: feeling that you are supposed to get something (usually something *nice*) just by being born into a family.

FIRST FRIDAY CLUB: a monthly ritual at Hollar
Seeds that keeps family and co-workers friendly and
on the same page. Here is an example of what we
do:

> *We meet most months at 11:00 a.m. on the first
> Friday of the month. All Rocky Ford year-round
> staff members attend. We share good news and
> bad news. Anyone can give someone else a "thank
> you" in front of everyone. We talk about recent
> sales, and any complaints. Possible changes to our
> Procedure Manual are discussed before they are
> enacted. In order that the meeting gets started on
> time, we give tickets to those that are seated at
> 11:00. Two are drawn for family dinners at a
> favorite local restaurant.*

IMPASSABLE STONE: when a founder or other business owner has the largest part of his estate tied up
in the business; creates problems if founder dies suddenly — no one in the family can afford to inherit
the company, too much inheritance tax is due, there
is no money with which to pay the tax. Also applies
to the situation when owner starts to write his first
will and tries to divide his estate equally and/or fairly to his heirs?

INSTITUTIONALIZE: take something good, but
because you repeat it at unnecessary times it
becomes bad

INTRA-PRENEURSHIP: when a company uses the talent of their creative employees to develop innovative products and services

INTUITIVE TRUST: you know your family members, you know what to expect from them

NEPOTISM: hiring a family member (It got me where I am today!)

NEPOTISM POLICY: A policy that outlines how family members will be hired. See page 127 for a sample.

NUCLEAR FAMILY: a husband, wife, and their kids

SAFETY NET: something like a trampoline, at a circus it sits under the high wire or trapeze acts; saves a messy clean-up in case of unexpected falls

STEWARDSHIP: the feeling instilled by The Legacy Speech; promotes the ideal that the owners of the family business aren't the owners, just caretakers.

SWEAT EQUITY: what you earn by way of your own work, not family favoritism.

THE LEGACY SPEECH: used to promote the idea that the business should stay in the family for perpetuity. This is either a wonderful way to try to insure that the business will continue for generations, or it is a device to enslave someone to your ideals, depending on your point of view.

TRIANGULATION: Johnny goes to Daddy and tattles on Maggie; Daddy punishes Maggie; Maggie explains that Johnny started it; Daddy punishes Johnny — Wouldn't it be better for Daddy to stay out of the triangle and let the other two settle it?

VISION: mythical ability to see the future

About the Author

While representing his family business on trips to over 20 countries, Larry Hollar always turns the conversation with other family business people with a question. "What is it like working with your family every day?" Or, "Which comes first for you, the business or the family?"

Such conversations have led to informal consultations with many business families, which has spurred Larry on to more study of the family business system. Ideas from many sources are tested in his business, then either discarded or incorporated. After years of working for his father, cooperating with his brothers and mentoring his sons, Larry has lived through the transitions that all family businesses go through.

Hollar lives in La Junta, Colorado, with his wife Helen Hollar, and within a holler's distance of many other family businesses.

To Order More Copies . . .

Please send me _____ copies of *Keep Your Business Close and Your Family Closer* for $14.95 a copy, plus $3.00 shipping and handling for one book. (Add $1.00 for each additional book, up to 10 books.) Colorado residents add 45¢ sales tax, per book. Total amount _____.

Name _____

Address _____

City _____

State _____ Zip Code _____

Daytime phone number: _____

Make checks payable to Piñon Publishing.

Piñon Publishing
140 West 29th #197 • Pueblo, Colorado 81008
phone: 866-851-6305 • fax: 888-726-9038
online: www.fambizjuggler.com